A Study of Omaha Indian Music

A Study of Omaha Indian Music

By Alice C. Fletcher
Aided by Francis La Flesche

Introduction by Helen Myers

University of Nebraska Press
Lincoln and London

The paper in this book meets the minimum requirements of American National Standard for Information Sciences—Permanence of
Paper for Printed Library Materials, ANSI z39.48-1984

First Bison Book printing: 1994
Most recent printing indicated by the last digit below:
10   9   8   7   6   5   4   3   2   1

Library of Congress Cataloging-in-Publication Data
Fletcher, Alice C. (Alice Cunningham), 1838–1923.
A study of Omaha Indian music / by Alice C. Fletcher, aided by
Francis La Flesche; introduction by Helen Myers.—Bison book ed.
    p.   cm.
Originally published: Cambridge, Mass.: Peabody Museum of Amer-
ican Archaeology and Ethnology, 1893. (Archaeological and eth-
nological papers of the Peabody Museum; v. 1, no. 5). With new
introd.
"Omaha songs" (with piano acc.): p.
ISBN 0-8032-6887-4
1. Omaha Indians—Music—History and criticism.   I. La Flesche,
Francis, d. 1932.   II. Title.   III. Series: Archaeological and ethnological papers of the Peabody Museum; vol. 1, no. 5.
ML3557.F61   1994
781.62'975—dc20
94-26951   CIP
MN

Originally published in the Archaeological and Ethnological Papers
of the Peabody Museum, Harvard University, Vol. 1, No. 5, June
1893.

To
Mrs. Mary Copley Thaw,
whose unfailing interest in these researches has made
possible the completion of the work,
this monograph on Omaha Indian Music
is gratefully dedicated.

INTRODUCTION

by Helen Myers

aided by Elsie Myers-Stainton

It is thus near to Nature that much of the life of the Indian still is; hence its story, rather than being replete with statistics of commercial conquest, is a record of the Indian's relations with and his dependence on the phenomena of the universe—the trees and shrubs, the sun and stars, the lightning and rain—for these to him are animate creatures.

> Edward S. Curtis,
> *The North American Indians*

Alice Cunningham Fletcher (1838–1923), in persevering as she did to live among the Omaha Indians, showed a pioneering spirit that also characterized her writings about Native American music. Her involvement with the Omahas began in 1879 at a meeting of a Boston literary society where she was introduced to the Omaha singer Francis La Flesche, who became a lifelong informant, confidant, and collaborator. She first visited the Omahas in 1881 and returned again and again in the next three decades, during which time she photographed and recorded (first by ear and later with the Edison cylinder machine) Indian folkways. These primary source materials demonstrated her empathy for the Omahas and her understanding of them.

A Study of Omaha Indian Music

The present volume contains Alice Fletcher's *A Study of Omaha Indian Music* (1893), including ninety-two songs, all from the Omaha tribe in Nebraska. In an essay of fifty-one pages, she describes and classifies these songs and with the encouragement and assistance of Omaha singer Francis La Flesche places this music in its cultural context. Based on personal contact with the performers on their own ground, this revealing analysis was immediately recognized as "a most valuable contribution to our knowledge of the music and poetry of primitive people" (Boas, 1894, p. 168). One hundred and one years later it is still regarded as a most valuable source about the life of early American Indian tribes. She noted then that "the Omahas as a tribe have ceased to exist" (p. 57). Students now can be grateful that devoted, indomitable spirits like Alice Fletcher hurried to preserve a record of that vanishing culture.

Included also in the present book, as in the original publication by the Peabody Museum of Harvard University, is "A Report on the Structural Peculiarities of the Music," nineteen pages in which John Comfort Fillmore explains his theory of harmonization for the Indian tunes that he has scored here for piano.

What gives Alice Fletcher's account of this Omaha Indian music its special appeal, and value, is that she places the music in its setting. She shows the importance of that music in Indian life—in the communal tribal life of the Omahas and in the individual lives of tribal members. Music, chiefly singing, is part of every event—of ceremonies honoring the sun, the corn, and animals, of rites preparing for war, of social gatherings for games and sport, of communal decision-making, of personal crises giving expression to fear, sorrow, joy, love, religious feeling. As she says, "Among the Indians, music envelopes like an atmosphere every religious, tribal and social ceremony as well as every personal experience" (p. 10). Songs also serve to preserve the history of the tribe: "The songs of a tribe are its heritage" (p. 10).

The charm of Fletcher's writing about the Native American scene in her day (and make no mistake about it, her voice is beguiling) lies in the perceived authenticity of her stories and in the obvious rapport she achieved with these—then, perhaps still—exotic people. She not only lived among them, she understood the why of their customs, especially their singing. She understood also the weight of injustice done them, and this sympathy shines in her telling of their life. Understanding and sympathy can hardly be outweighed in progressing toward knowledge. Here we have both.

First Fieldwork: A Transformational Experience

Alice Fletcher contested the generally accepted theories of her day about the "savage" music of the Native American peoples. What music she heard after months of study contradicted the theories:

> My first studies were crude and full of difficulties, difficulties that I afterward learned were bred of preconceived ideas, the influence of generally accepted theories concerning "savage" music. The tones, the scales, the rhythms, the melodies that I heard, which after months of work stood out more and more clearly as indisputable facts, lay athwart these theories and could not be made to coincide with them. For a considerable time I was more inclined to distrust my ears than my theories, but when I strove to find facts that would agree with these theories I met only failure. Meanwhile the Indians sang on. . . .

In July 1883, Fletcher suffered a severe and painful illness (inflammatory rheumatism or rheumatoid arthritis). She was taken to the Presbyterian Omaha mission, where she lay near death for five weeks. Then she was moved by wagon to the Winnebago agency headquarters, where she remained for eight months, still gravely ill. While there, her Indian friends cared for her in, she says, "affectionate solicitude" and "sang softly because I was weak, and there was no drum, and then it was that the distraction of noise and confusion of theory were dispelled, and the sweetness, the beauty and meaning of these songs were revealed to me" (p. 8).

Picture the young Francis La Flesche (he was twenty-seven) singing his cherished Omaha songs for this brave white woman, who had been stricken while struggling to help his people. By the time she had recovered (ever after, she walked with a cane), surely an unusual bond had been formed.

Her recovery was then celebrated with the Wa-wa*n* ceremony. (The italicized *n* is to express a nasal sound.) The first white person to observe the Omaha ceremony, she describes it elegantly—including the "Pipe" or "Calumet" dance. She also notated and transcribed some two dozen of its songs and explains: "The highly poetic character of the Wa-wa*n* songs and of this entire ceremony is native; nothing has been borrowed from our own race that I have been able to discover. The ethical teachings are in strict accordance with Indian ideals which here reach some of their highest expressions" (p. 38). The reader may wish to consult recordings of this repertory made by Fletcher and La Flesche on cylinder during subsequent field trips, 1895–97, available on Library of Congress Disk AFC L71. The "Song of Approach" from the WaWa*n*, recorded in 1896, is on Side 1, band 4; see Lee and Vigna, 1985. The recording also includes three songs of the Hethu'shka Society (in *A Study of Omaha Indian Music*, pp. 25–33, 86–99), examples of the He'dewachi or "Tribal Dance" (pp. 19–21, 82), a "Funeral Song" (pp. 42, 122), "Ritual of the Maize," Mi'kaci or Wolf songs" (pp. 44–45, 123–26), Na'gthe Waa*n* or "Captive Songs" (pp. 45–46, 126–29), "Rally Songs," two Wewa'chi or Victory Dance Songs (pp. 47–48, 134–36), the Ho*n*'Hewachi or "Night Dance Society Songs," and examples of Wau'Waa*n* or "Woman Song" (pp. 52–53, 143–45) and Bice'waa*n* "Love Song" (p. 150).

The Omaha Repertory

Fletcher classified the several hundred songs she collected and transcribed. A group of songs designated as Wa-zhi*n*-thae-thae are sung, she reports, with the purpose of giving "strength, power, passion" to the warrior in battle (p. 46). In another group, songs of triumph, the movements are told of a man "carefully making his way through the tall prairie grass, avoiding observation that he may successfully capture the horses of his enemy" (p. 48). Some individual songs are regarded as private property and have been handed down for generations. Some are bought and sold.

Fletcher, the scholar-scientist, endeavored to date this music: of a song she reckoned to be very old, she says, "The most aged men to be found in the tribe ten years ago, had heard it when they were boys sung by old warriors" (p. 28). Fletcher, the poet-ethnomusicologist, says of another song, "I have heard old men sing this song in a low tone as they sat by the fire, tears in their faded eyes, their thoughts upon the friends who had gone, and the days that could never return" (p. 29). Another song, expressing the thought that the lives of persons are at the command of the gods, she says dates back to the early part of the nineteenth century and probably came down from the eighteenth century.

To Fletcher the Indian music she heard was "faithful to the thought." One song suggests "the eagle stirring, and lifting itself from the nest; as the wind blows the branches of the trees" (p. 38). Another suggests "sunshine, birds and verdure, and a fleet, happy movement" (p. 42). In another, sung while the box elder wood is charred upon the fire (for the purpose of blackening a warrior's face), "the music expresses the eagerness of the warrior and suggests the tremulous movement of the leaves just before a thunder storm" (p. 26).

Throughout the book Fletcher translates Indian thoughts into her own emotional terms. Ethnomusicologists now endeavor (in futility, one might ask) to avoid such a transfer since it lays down value judgments. And in using figurative language, as she does, Western values are certainly expressed: "The music is as simple and untutored as the flowers that are often the only listeners" (p. 53). Here the taint of the evolutionary theory of the day as applied to music has encroached upon her analysis: the song does not come from a simple and untutored culture.

Indeed, Fletcher seems to have been pulled by the power of evolutionary thinking in part away from her own feeling and from what her studies revealed, that the Omaha cultural context was not simple or savage. In the concluding paragraphs of her essay, she gives a clear example of social evolutionism as applied to music: "With the Indian, labor was *not yet* divorced from supernatural influences. . . . The ground was *still* Mother Earth. . . . The Indian had *not shaken himself* free . . . ; he had *not yet* comprehended. . . . (p. 57, emphases added). Fletcher describes her task as "the archaeology of music" (p. 57) and pictures herself metaphorically as digging back to an earlier time to a music, not primitive, but hampered by "the limit which the Omaha Indian's environment placed upon the development of his mental life and expression" (p. 57). Here is a wonderful, readable account of the theory of social evolution applied to music, that is, Darwin applied to society—a stance, however, that is never used in modern ethnomusicology. A clear example of an earlier theory. Students, don't read *about* it—read it.

Nevertheless, Fletcher held throughout to ethnomusicology's basic tenet, a simple and fundamental idea about music and culture, a pioneering idea in her time, now taken for granted: "The music, to be understood and appreciated, needs its original setting" (p. 55).

The Collection Process

The present collection of ninety-two songs was initially notated in the field and in Washington D.C. by Fletcher, who, without the aid of a cylinder recorder, surely asked her informants to repeat lines many times until the transcription of text and tune was complete. This painstaking process had been the only method of collection prior to the invention of the Edison phonograph in 1877.

Soon after the phonograph was invented, cylinders were used by German ethnologists to record samples of music in imperial outposts. These field materials were delivered to the Berlin laboratory, the Psychological Institute, for analysis by Carl Stumpf (1848–1936), Otto Abraham (1872–1926), and Erich von Hornbostel (1877–1936). This team, and Hornbostel in particular, published hundreds of articles, often appended to hefty ethnographic studies to present non-Western music to the Western world. These researchers were particularly interested in non-Western musical samples as they might shed light on their universal theories of the relations of stimulus and sensation, musical perception, and binaural hearing. This methodology—analysis of material collected in the field by others—is now called "armchair ethnomusicology."

Alice Fletcher's point of view was immeasurably different. She was interested in the role of music in the lives of people. What she did that was decisively important, she went to live with them. This kind of move is now known as fieldwork.

By the early 1890s, other American ethnologists were using the phonograph to record Native American music in the field: Jesse Walter Fewkes (1850–1930), the Passamaquoddy Indian songs in 1890; James Mooney (1861–1921), Caddoan songs in 1895; Franz Boas (1858–1942), Kwakiutl music in 1893, as well as George Bird Grinnell (1849–1938) and Walter McClintock (1870–1949), who recorded several years later in Montana. The Fletcher–La Flesche cylinder collection dates probably from September 1895 with the sixteen ritual songs recorded by La Flesche (Lee and La Vigna, 1985). Although the full extent of the collection is uncertain, the team recorded over 90 cylinders of Omaha material in Nebraska and in Washington between 1895 and 1905. Lee and La Vigna mention that Fletcher recorded some 150 more cylinders of Plains material and La Flesche some 254 cylinders relating to his research with the Osage people, also of the Great Plains.

Textual Analysis

Songs texts posed a particular problem for Fletcher. Words were sometimes modified, accents changed, and extra syllables added to fit the rhythm of the music. This practice made transcription and translation difficult. In particular, Fletcher struggled with the interpretation of non-lexical vocables, which constitute a large proportion of the texts. She says: "A majority of the songs . . . are furnished almost wholly with syllables which are not parts or even fragments of words but sounds that lend themselves easily to singing and are without definite meaning"

(p. 12). But she notes the unchanging use of vocables and assumes they are important. She observes that the initial letter is generally *h, th,* or *y,* the syllables are vowel sounds both open and nasal, and goes on to report that they seem to be used as an expression of feeling. The *h* and *th* sounds show "gentler emotions" such as love, sadness, and idealistic aspiration, she suggests; the *y* shows "sharp explosive tones," warlike emotions.

Modern ethnomusicologists are still wrestling with the nonlexical vocables in these songs. Formerly called "meaningless" or "nonsense" syllables (for example by Boas himself), scholars now say, yes, they mean something; this a lively topic for research in the 1990s (Myers, 1993, p. 409). But Fletcher deserves full credit for assuming they mean something, and for searching for this meaning. And in this regard Fletcher introduces a new concept; she speaks of a "composer" who "set syllables to his song" (p. 12). So she considers these Indians to be composers (certainly not savages) and not a social group whose music is a result of communal creation, an earlier theory of "folk" composition.

Fletcher reports that the instruments used to accompany Omaha song were few, drums and rattles, but they could produce a tremendous sound. The large drums formerly were made of a hollowed tree section, tuned by filling partly with water, the skin moistened and stretched to tone. This type was almost unknown in Fletcher's day. She saw kegs used instead. Formerly large flat drums were made by stretching a calf skin over a hoop, but are now replaced by "ordinary drums" (p. 54). The large drum sticks were covered with skins at the ends. Small drums were beaten with the fingers. Rattles were made of hollowed gourds filled with small or larger stones. To some ears and to Fletcher's at first, the singing was lost in "overpowering noise" (p. 71). The other Omaha instrument, the whistle or flageolet, is generally not used to accompany singing except in love songs. This type of "courting flute" is widely distributed among Indian groups. Its distinctive organological feature is an external duct whereby the airstream is directed outside the tube and immediately back in via a wooden block mounted over the air hole, splitting the air and creating musical sound (Riemer-Weller, 1984). The volume includes two flageolet melodies (nos. 91 and 92).

Musical Analysis: Fillmore

The Victorian anthropologists generally shied away from analysis of the music they collected, regarding such efforts as particular to the science of music. Ethnologists turned instead to musicians for analysis of the musical sounds, the successful formation of a like-minded team determining to a large extent the success of the outcome. Fletcher's first assistant was John Comfort Fillmore (1843–98), a teacher at the Milwaukee School of Music, who had studied in Leipzig, Germany, and at Oberlin. That Fletcher did not have the use of a phonograph on her first trip becomes an intriguing and incalculable issue in the bitter debate that erupted in the mid-1890s between Fletcher's assistant, Fillmore, and Fewkes's assistant, Benjamin Ives Gilman.

Fillmore, who distrusted the phonograph, was happy enough to work with Fletcher's transcriptions taken down by ear. He held to the theory that there existed a common harmonic foundation for all musics, and that the Omaha discrepancy of pitch (which could not be repeated and tested without an actual recording to replay) could be accounted for by what he regarded as a fact that the American Indians had a "primitive," "savage," inferior sense of pitch discrimination. Fillmore's method was only partially successful and is no longer used.

Fillmore found the scoring of Fletcher's transcriptions especially difficult because the Indians had no standard pitch as, for example, the modern Western practice that the A above middle C has 440 vibrations per second. The Omahas sang in unison; but with two or three octaves accommodated by both men and women singing together (sometimes using falsetto), a sort of harmonics seemed to be achieved. Fillmore scored Alice Fletcher's notations and transcriptions, and arranged the songs for piano, supplying what he reckoned to be the "latent harmony" of this—for him—primitive music. He tested his chords against the Indians' perception of the songs, using a number of informants, and settled on those harmonics claimed by his subjects to be most pleasing to Indian ears.

Songs as notated for the piano are included here to illustrate Fletcher's observations about the music. She tells us one needs to learn to appreciate the Indian style of singing. Although the songs here are scored for piano, Fletcher argues that since Indian music does not lend itself to any scale, a violin could better have sounded the chromatics, tremolo, and slurs of the singers. So evidently she expected that Fillmore's renditions could not be perfect.

A further problem in the transcription and scoring for piano was the preferred Omaha singing style that favors using vocal "vibrations" ("pulsations" in Nettl, 1954). Fletcher writes, "If, when I was learning one of these songs, I held a quarter or half note to a steady tone, I was corrected and told to 'make it tremble'" (p. 15). Further: "The Indian is apt to slur from the pitch; he seldom attacks a note clearly" (p. 152).

Fillmore endeavored to reduce the Indian songs to a pentatonic major scale or a corresponding minor scale, but as he comments, "There remained some very puzzling cases of songs whose tones could not be reduced to either major or minor scale" (pp. 60–61). He had a problem also where Indians sang the note "about a quarter of tone above the pitch," which he tried to resolve by "syncopation" (p. 109).

Another problem for Fillmore concerned the notation of Omaha rhythm: "One of the most striking peculiarities of rhythm is the mixture of twos and threes in the same measure" (p. 67). But he ends up admiringly: "Rhythm is by far the most elaborately developed element of the Indian music, and in this respect civilized music has not surpassed it, at least in the point of combining dissimilar rhythms" (p. 68).

He also struggled over unconventional phrasing, which, he says, has a "rich variety" (p. 68) with anywhere from two to seven measures to a phrase. Indeed Fillmore ran into so many "puzzling cases," one wonders why it did not occur to him that the Western highway he had chosen might not give access to Indian trails. Indian singing sounds harsh. The women have loud, shrill voices. The men often shout. All singers are competing with loud drumming. Under these conditions Fillmore claims it would be impossible to achieve beauty of tone: "Men sang *forte* and *fortissimo* for hours together, out of doors, in the face of a strong southeast wind, with an accompaniment of big drum and rattles" (p. 70).

Fillmore's struggles with notation, with pitch, rhythm, and phrasing, however lacking in precision, do provide insights into the special qualities of Omaha music: "This Indian music is the true and natural expression of genuine emotion; much of it profound, much of it high and ennobling; and the better it is known the more this will be seen" (p. 71). The defects he sees are no beauty of tone and uncertainty of intonation or wavering pitch. The merits he sees are elaborate rhythms and the spontaneous expression of emotion. Bruno Nettl (1954) describes the vocal usage of this region: "The vocal technique of the Plains-Pueblo area was considered by Hornbostel to be radically inherent among all Indians, since it is found also in South America. It is characterized by a great deal of tension in the vocal organs which is sustained throughout a song, an effort to sing as loudly as possible, and pulsation on the longer tones. Strong accents, glissandos, and as a result, intonation which is probably less stable or fixed than that of the other musical areas, as well as ornamentation and shouting before, during, and after songs are the main results of this tension" (p. 24).

For several decades now the Plains Indian's style has become the preferred one in the Pan-Indian movement; you hear it in powwows all over the nation. Indians themselves have chosen this style as the most distinctively Indian, perhaps because it sounds the least Western.

The ethnologists early on the scene came upon this difficult type. What they found was indeed perplexing and most of the ensuing stereotypical mimicry perpetuated by whites, sold by Hollywood (cowboys and Injuns), is directed at this Plains type. Fletcher was not mistaken in puzzlement: modern research bears out the difficulty of studying this deceptively simple musical style.

A Bitter Debate

Fillmore's harmonizations were bitterly criticized at the time. His efforts and theories were challenged by Benjamin Ives Gilman (1852–1933), a psychologist, who transcribed and analyzed phonograph cylinders (the first in the history of ethnomusicology, then called comparative musicology) collected

by Jesse Walter Fewkes among the Zuñi and Hopi Indians
(1890).

Totally rejecting Fillmore's theory of latent harmony,
Gilman published Indian songs without key or time signa-
tures; he ridiculed Fillmore's use of Western notation and used
a forty-five-line "quarter-tone" staff. Working with cylinder
recordings, Gilman noted in his daily laboratory notes the
speed of the cylinder machine (resulting in change in the abso-
lute pitch on playback), the condition of the batteries that ran
the machine, as well as other details of his methodology. In this
manner he sought through scientific method to reduce, perhaps eliminate, Western bias in an objective study of non-Western tonal systems based on observation and not theory. "The
step taken is no other than that separating the indicative from
the imperative mood, the real from the ideal. Written music as
otherwise known is not a record of occurrence but of purpose. . . . [My] Zuñi notation . . . gave memoranda of observation. . . . The present notations . . . report similar facts. . . .
Compared with the customary writing of music, these again
are as annals [of a country's history] to laws, as a ship's log to its
sailing directions" (Gilman, 1908, pp. 8–9; quoted by Ellingson
in Myers, 1992, p. 123). All this shows an approach much more
sophisticated than Fillmore's.

On the other hand, a review by Franz Boas—noted ethnolo-
gist and colleague of Fillmore, and a leading force in the development of American anthropology who argued for fieldwork
over armchair theorizing—gave the book and Fillmore's analysis high marks: "The present collection of songs and tunes of
the Omaha Indians is a most valuable contribution to our
knowledge of the music and poetry of primitive people." He
adds from his own experience: "Miss Fletcher's statement, that
every phase of the Indian's life is made a subject of song and
poetry, is borne out by the evidence accumulated from all parts
of our continent. She also emphasized the frequency of traditional songs which have been handed down from unknown
generations." And: "Miss Fletcher explains the curious trans-
formations of words and the introduction of numerous meaningless syllables as an effort towards poetic expression in measured language, and this explanation is certainly correct."

Himself a noted researcher of Kwakiutl and Inuit music, Boas says: "Her views on the briefness of Indian songs are also worthy of attention. The Indian does not actually express his emotions in the song, but merely intimates them." And: "To this might be added that the traditional songs refer to beliefs and theories which are known to every member of the tribe, or are not intended to be understood by the uninitiated" (pp. 168–71).

Boas approves of Fillmore's report on the structural peculiarities of the Indian music as important for understanding "primitive music," and of Fillmore's judgment that a sense of key relationship and of harmonic relations is "at least subconsciously present in the Indian mind." Boas agrees "that Indians have a deficient intonation . . . but that when the songs are repeated to them correctly . . . accompanied by natural harmonies, they enjoy them and express themselves satisfied with the reproduction."

"The reviewer had the pleasure of repeating these experiments in company with Mr. Fillmore, and he is perfectly satisfied that Mr. Fillmore's is correct."

Fillmore, a piano teacher, based his appreciation of music and his theories about music on the piano keyboard—at a time when the piano was the main vehicle for making music in many homes. The student of piano at the time learned about scales, rhythm, tone, and about a theory of Western music concerned with a keyboard, black and white keys. When notes showed up (as in the Omaha songs) that, as it were, fell between the cracks of the piano keyboard, such tones were described as out of tune. Thus Fillmore readily declared that the Indians were deficient in tone perception and he set out to delineate what he figured they *meant* to sing (Fillmore, 1895).

But pity all those beleaguered Indians who were trying to cooperate. Their own vocal material was being played back to them on a piano. How different piano strings from human vocal chords! What a different sound! Then they were asked "many times" ("I have myself personally repeated this experiment many times," p. 61). And sympathize with the agreeable La Flesche ("I tried numerous experiments on Mr. La Flesche," who, confronted by the satisfied transcriber, must choose between unsatisfactory alternatives: "His comments would run about thus: 'This sounds right to me up to that point; the next part is weak; now it is better,—but it isn't right yet; now it is right'" [p. 65]).

Although Fillmore felt the Indians must have a "latent" sense of harmony, on the matter of scales, he finally gave up: "I am forced to the conclusion that melody is a product of the natural harmonic sense and that all efforts to reduce primitive melodies to scales without reference to the natural harmonies implied in them must prove futile. I therefore spare myself the useless labor of enumerating all the specific varieties of scale to be found in these songs, regarding it as a wholly irrelevant matter" (pp. 61–62).

With such a declaration, Fillmore rejected the most recent findings of his day on non-Western tunings, in particular those of the eminent English physicist and phonetician, Alexander J. Ellis. Ellis had examined the scales of non-diatonic, non-harmonic tonal systems, including examples from Siam, Europe, Africa, and Asia, for example of the Javanese gamelan (orchestra). To aid in the precise measurement of pitch, he developed the "cents" system whereby each semitone is divided into one hundred cents. The pronouncement he read before the Royal Society in 1885 as a consequence of his investigations has become somewhat of a credo for modern ethnomusicology, that "the Musical Scale is not one, not 'natural,' nor even founded necessarily on the laws of the constitution of musical sound, so beautifully worked out by Helmholtz, but very diverse, very artificial, and very capricious" (p. 526). This finding, which led the way for a more rational cross-cultural comparison of tonal systems, was rejected by Fillmore, who favored Helmholtz's earlier theory of a universal and "natural" musical scale based on Western musical perception (Helmholtz, 1863).

Fillmore's mention of the "Modern Romantic School" (p. 62) with reference to Beethoven, Schubert, and others in order to stress his contention that Indians have only latent perception of musical relationships illustrates a fairly common stance that is now rejected by ethnomusicologists—a stance that, like so many earlier notions in anthropology, presumed the supremacy of white folks.

Around the turn of the century, in response to the concerns of comparative musicologists regarding a uniform transcription process—as so vividly illustrated with the Fillmore-Gilman debate on the transcription of Indian melody—Otto Abraham and Erich von Hornbostel of the Berlin Psychological Institute published "Vorshläge für die Transkription exotischer Melodien" ("Proposals for the Transcription of Exotic Melodies," 1909). As Ellingson points out: "Hornbostel and Abraham faced the apparent paradox that Fillmore's transcriptions were musically clear and comprehensive but distorted musical truth, while Gilman's were precise and objective, but obscured musicality by their complexity. Their solution was 'a compromise between fluent legibility and objective precision' (1909, p. 2) that incorporated aspects of both approaches into a redefined synthesis" (in Myers, 1992, p. 125).

Having thus put Fillmore in his place, the ethnomusicologist must stress the importance of reading his work as an original source. The researcher may have read about Fillmore, but any contemporary ethnomusicologist will be bowled over by Fillmore's actual words. Certainly the reading of primary sources is more revealing than reading about them. And we ask how could it be that one hundred and one years later we perceive that he is so wrong and she—Fletcher—so right. Both were of their time and both went to the Indians. But the student will see upon reading the original that whereas Fletcher was gifted in dealing with cultural diversity, Fillmore failed and was even prepared to change a pitch a semitone upward or downward to ensure its proper position in Western functional harmony. Perhaps he wished, like many late Romantics, for proof that music indeed is a universal language. Ironically, his work reveals that it is not.

Fillmore's method has become part of the history of ethnomusicology in its struggle to cope with the varying musics of the world. For that reason his essay deserves to be reprinted and to be read by students of ethnomusicology so that they may understand the changing methods and altered attitudes. Curiously, Fillmore acknowledges that without the help of Francis La Flesche his own investigations would have been impossible.

The Timely and the Enduring in Ethnomusicology

This timely reprint reminds us that little has changed. After a generation of studies concerned with scholarly objectivity, from the 1960s to the early 1980s, scholars are once again acknowledging that subjectivity is inescapable and, moreover, that however much they might struggle to be a "fly on the wall" (would this be fair to people under investigation?) their mere presence alters the conditions of work and hence the music being studied. Reflexivity, the interaction between observer and observed, has since the late 1980s been taken into account by the forward-looking scholars in anthropology and ethnomusicology. The world is not a scientific laboratory (ironically, scientists have long maintained that even the laboratory is contaminated by personal bias, by accidental discovery, by serendipity). The central concern then and now of ethnomusicologists is living with people and gaining insight into their values. Fletcher affected her Indian friends and they her. She admits her preconceived ideas; she doesn't claim to go in with an open mind.

The distinction between the humanities and the sciences is not clear in the social sciences and especially in ethnomusicology (most vulnerable, because it deals with the most abstract manifestation of expressive culture). Only in recent years has the Society for Ethnomusicology been invited to join the American Council of Learned Societies. Now that a certain respectability has been achieved for this fledgling discipline, modern ethnomusicologists have felt able to confess, as did Alice Fletcher, the very personal nature of their research.

The Life of Alice Fletcher

Alice Cunningham Fletcher happened to be born in Cuba in 1838, where her parents had gone because of her father's ill health (he died the next year of tuberculosis). Fletcher attended exclusive schools, traveled in Europe, and taught at several private schools. With a pleasing voice and attractive manner, she was successful on the lecture circuits, and thereby supported herself. While preparing lectures about ancient

Americans, she met Frederick W. Putnam, director of the Peabody Museum at Harvard, who encouraged her to continue anthropological study and stressed a scientific approach to the study. For a time she was an assistant at the Museum.

Fletcher met Francis La Flesche (1857–1932) at a Boston fund-raising event in the fall of 1879. "Frank," as she later called him, was the son of the Omaha chief Joseph La Flesche. Susette, Francis's sister, was interpreter for Standing Bear, the Ponca chief. Along with Thomas Henry Tibbles, a Nebraska journalist who later married Susette, they were touring the East to protest removal of the Poncas from the Dakota Territory.

Having lectured chiefly on material gathered in libraries, Fletcher now wished for first-hand information. Early in 1881, she contacted Susette and Tibbles, who during the summer arranged for her to return with them to the Omaha reservation in Nebraska. That fall they traveled there in a wooden wagon and then continued on into Sioux Territory. This was the beginning. The result is described by her mentor, Frederick Putnam, in his Editorial Note to the present book: "Her long residence among the Indians and her success in winning their love and perfect confidence have enabled her to penetrate the meaning of many things which to an ordinary observer of Indian life are incomprehensible" (p. 1).

Again early in 1882, while working for the Omahas in Washington, she frequently sought Francis La Flesche's help. They helped each other thereafter for more than forty years.

Alice and Francis worked together and maintained a caring and affectionate relationship for all those years. She informally adopted him as her son, a move apparently made to ensure that he could inherit her estate. When government work kept them both in Washington, D.C., they shared her home there. They were devoted to each other and dependent on each other.

It is fruitless to speculate on how much Francis La Flesche contributed to Alice Fletcher's success. Doubtless his help was invaluable, as hers to him. Like many a fortuitous combination, these two gifted persons formed an ethnographic team that was greater than the sum of it parts.

In addition to her visits to various Indian reservations,

Fletcher was more than busy. She continued to write. She became an intermediary between government agencies and Indian tribes. She was asked to administer settlements of controversial land allotments. She sponsored educational projects for Indians. She was a vice president of the American Association for the Advancement of Science (1896), a founding member of the American Anthropological Association (1902), president of the American Folklore Society (1905), and was on the editorial board of the *American Anthropologist* (1899–1916).

In *The Century Magazine* of January 1894, there appeared Alice Fletcher's "Indian Songs; Personal Studies of Indian Life." The article is a pleasant piece, illustrated with two engravings and notation for three songs. The text is similar to her *Study of Omaha Indian Music,* including a number of identical passages, but for the *Century* it is enlivened with comments on the colorful dress of the Indians (red, green, and yellow blankets, "touches of vermilion upon the cheeks, their ear-ornaments of white shell hung nearly to their waists"—p. 422), and such details as being "alert to catch the rattle of a disturbed snake" (p. 421).

To the ethnomusicologist, most revealing is her comment about her fright at the first sight in Dakota Territory of the Indians assembled for a dance and her suffering over their musical performance: "I have since had many a laugh with my red friends over this my first and only fright, caused, as I now know, by the unconscious influence of the popular idea of 'Injuns'; but it was long after this initiation before my ears were able to hear in Indian music little besides a screaming downward movement that was gashed and torn by the vehemently beaten drum" (vol. 48, p. 422)—the last thirteen words are also used on the first page of *Omaha Indian Music.*

In fact, this article had been put together and sent off posthaste to the magazine with Fletcher's hope of being the first in print with such an ethnographic study. But *Century* did not publish the article until after the book had appeared. Thus Benjamin Ives Gilman beat her into print (1891) with his analysis of the wax cylinder recorded by Jesse Walter Fewkes of Zuñi melodies. This research was financed by Mary Thaw Hemenway, "a major stockholder in the Edison company," as Dorothy Sara Lee says, "who wished to test the phonograph's usefulness for ethnographic work, and who probably furnished the machine" (in Myers, 1993, p. 21).

Fillmore's article, "A Study of Indian Music," was published in the *Century* a month after Fletcher's (February 1894). In it, he uses without explanation, ten examples of Omaha songs as numbered in the book.

A Study of Omaha Indian Music is dedicated to Mrs. Mary Thaw of Pittsburgh, who in 1890 established a lifetime fellowship for Fletcher at the Peabody Museum. Mrs. Thaw also purchased in 1892 a house for her in Washington at 214 First Street SE. This home became a gathering place for intellectuals, among them Ainsworth Spofford, President Lincoln's secretary, later Librarian of Congress. Fletcher lived there, with La Flesche, until her death in 1923.

At her death, aged eighty-five, Alice Fletcher had been in the public eye for more than forty years—as lecturer, author, government official, anthropologist, and musicologist. She worked hard and welcomed the rewards, chiefly recognition of her accomplishments, which at other times she felt was denied her. She was brave, determined, resourceful, and most important of all, she left a legacy of some forty-six writings on aspects of Indian life and music.

A Study of Omaha Indian Music was originally published as number 5, volume 1 of the Archaeological and Ethnological Papers of the Peabody Museum, Harvard University. It began on page 237 of volume 1.

*　*　*

From "Alice C. Fletcher," *Science*, vol. 58, no. 1494: (17 August 1923) p. 115:

"In the year 1881 there appeared on the Omaha reservation, in Nebraska, a white woman. She visited the Indians in their homes and began to make friends with them. At first they were not disposed to talk, but after a time it occurred to one to ask: 'Why are you here?' She replied: 'I came to learn, if you will let me, something about your tribal organization, social customs, tribal rites, traditions and songs. Also to see if I can help you in any way.'

"At the suggestion of help the faces of the Indians bright-ened with hope. The Indian continued: 'You have come at a time when we are in distress. We have learned that the "land paper" given us by the Great Father does not make us secure in our homes; that we could be ousted and driven to the Indian Territory as the Poncas were. We want a "strong paper." We are told that we can get one through an act of Congress. Can you help us?'

"The little woman replied: 'Bring me your "land paper" and come prepared to tell me about your home and the size of the land you have in cultivation. Come soon.' The news spread and the Indians came. . . .

". . . This brave, unselfish woman was Alice C. Fletcher, whom the Omahas learned to love.

". . . Miss Fletcher came to Washington to help push the bill [to secure land titles for the Omahas] through. It passed both houses, was approved August 7, 1882, and became law.

"In April, 1883, Miss Fletcher was appointed special agent to carry out the provisions of the law. When she was about to begin her work the older members of the tribe came together for consultation as to how they could best express their gratitude for what she had done for the tribe. They decided to perform for her the ancient calumet ceremony, although it was not customary to give it informally. A notice was given to the people to come, and on the day appointed many came and assembled in an earth lodge. The calumets were set up in their sacred place, and when Miss Fletcher entered as the honored guest the house became silent. Three men arose and took up the symbolic pipes (the calumets) and the lynx skin on which they rested; then, standing side by side, they sang softly the opening song. At the close the three men turned, and facing the people, who sat in a wide circle, sang a joyful song as they moved around the circle, waving the sacred pipes over their heads. Song after song they sang for their friend, of the joy and happiness that would follow whem men learned to live together in peace. When the evening was over they told Miss Fletcher that she was free to study this or any other of their tribal rites.

"Miss Fletcher carried on her ethnological researches among the Omaha, Pawnee, Winnebago, Sioux, Nez Pierce and other tribes. She published many papers descriptive of the life and ceremonials of the tribes she studied. . . . Many of the ceremonial songs collected by Miss Fletcher have been used as themes by American composers, notably by Cadman, Farwell and others. . . .

"This great friend of the Indians was born in Cuba on the 15th day of March, 1838; on the evening of April 6, 1923, she passed away in her home, in Washington, D.C."

Francis La Flesche

Bibliography

Boas, Franz. "Review of *A Study of Omaha Indian Music*" in *Journal of American Folk-Lore* 7, no. 24 (Jan.–Mar. 1894): 168–71.

Brady, Erika, Maria La Vigna, Dorothy Sara Lee, and Thomas Vennum Jr. *The Federal Cylinder Project: A Guide to Field Cylinder Collections in Federal Agencies*. Vol. 1: *Introduction and Inventory. Studies in American Folklife*, no. 3, vol. 1. Washington DC: Library of Congress, 1984.

Densmore, Frances. "The Study of Indian Music in the Nineteenth Century." *American Anthropologist*, 29 (1927): 77–86.

———. "The Survival of Omaha Songs." *American Anthropologist* 46 (3): 418–20.

Dorson, James Owen. "Omaha Sociology." *Third Annual Report of the Smithsonian Institution Bureau of American Ethnology*, 1881–1882. Washington DC: United States Government Printing Office, 1884, 205–370.

Ellingson, Ter. "Transcription." In *Ethnomusicology: An Introduction*, ed. Helen Myers. London: Macmillan Press, 1992, 110–52.

Ellis, Alexander J. "On the Musical Scales of Various Nations." *Journal of the Royal Society of the Arts* (27 March 1885): 485–527 (30 October 1885): 1102–11.

Fillmore, John Comfort. "The Harmonic Structure of Indian Music." *American Anthropologist*, no. 1 (1899), 297–318.

———. "Primitive Scales and Rhythms." In *Memoirs. International Congress of Anthropologists*, ed. C. S. Wake. Chicago: Schulte, 1894, 158–75.

———. "Scales and Harmonies of Indian Music." *Music* 4 (1893), 478–89.

———. "A Study of Indian Music." *Century Magazine* 47 (1894), 616–23.

———. "What Do Indians Mean to Do When They Sing, and How Far

Do They Succeed?" *Journal of American Folk-lore* 8, no. 29 (1895), 138.

———. The Zuñi Music as Translated by Mr. Benjamin Ives Gilman." *Music* 5 (1893), 39–42.

Fletcher, Alice. "Historical Sketch of the Omaha Tribe of Indians in Nebraska." Washington DC: Bureau of Indian Affairs, 1885.

———. "Leaves from My Omaha Note-book." *Journal of American Folk-Lore* 2 (1889), 219–26.

———. "Indian Songs: Personal Studies of Indian Life." *Century Magazine* 47 (January 1894), 421–31.

———. *Indian Story and Song from North America*. Boston: Small, Maynard, 1900.

———. *The Hako: A Pawnee Ceremony*. With James R. Murie. Smithsonian Institution, Bureau of American Ethnology, 22nd Annual Report. Washington DC, 1904. 372 pp.

———. *The Omaha Tribe*. With Francis La Flesche. Smithsonian Institution, Bureau of American Ethnology, 27th Annual Report, 1905–1906. Washington DC, 1911. 672 pp.

———. *Indian Games and Dances with Native Songs Arranged from American Indian Ceremonials and Sports*. Boston: C. C. Birchard, 1915.

Gilman, Benjamin Ives. "Hopi Songs." *Journal of American Archaeology and Ethnology* 5 (1908), 1–26.

———. "Zuñi Melodies." *Journal of American Ethnology and Archaeology* 1 (1891), 65–91.

Helmholtz, H. *Die Lehre von den Tonempfindungen als psysiologische Grundlage für die Theorie der Musik*. Brunswick, 1863; English trans. by Alexander J. Ellis, as *On the Sensations of Tone as a Physiological Base for the Theory of Music*, 1875.

Hough, Walter. "Alice Cunningham Fletcher." *American Anthropologist* 25 (1923), 254–58.

La Flesche, Francis. "Alice C. Fletcher." *Science* 58, no. 1494 (17 August 1923), 115.

Lee, Dorothy Sara. "North America 1. Native American." In *Ethnomusicology: Historical and Regional Studies*, ed. Helen Myers. London: Macmillan Press, 1993, 19–36.

Lee, Dorothy Sara, and Maria La Vigna, eds. *Omaha Indian Music: Historical Recordings from the Fletcher/La Flesche Collection*. (Booklet accompanying Disk AFC L71) Washington DC: Library of Congress, 1985.

Lummis, Charles F. "In Memoriam: Alice C. Fletcher." *Art and Archaeology* 16 (1923), 75–76.

McNutt, J. C. "John Comfort Fillmore: A Student of Indian Music Reconsidered." *American Music* 2 (1984), 61.

Mark, Joan. *Four Anthropologists.* New York: Science History Publications, 1981.

———. *A Stranger in Her Native Land: Alice Fletcher and the American Indians.* Lincoln and London: University of Nebraska Press, 1988.

Merriam, Alan. *The Anthropology of Music.* Evanston: Northwestern University Press, 1964.

Myers, Helen, ed. *Ethnomusicology: An Introduction.* London: Macmillan Press, 1992.

———. *Ethnomusicology: Historical and Regional Studies.* London: Macmillan Press, 1993.

Nettl, Bruno. *North American Indian Musical Styles.* Philadelphia: American Folklore Society, 1954.

Pantaleoni, Hewitt. "A Reconsideration of Fillmore Reconsidered." *American Music* 3 (1985), 217–28.

Riemer-Weller, Mary. "Courting Flute." *The New Grove Dictionary of American Music.* Macmillan: London, 1984.

Welch, Rebecca Hancock. "Alice Cunningham Fletcher, Anthropologist and Indian Rights Reformer." Ph.D. diss., George Washington University, 1980.

Wilkins, Thurman. "Alice Cunningham Fletcher." In *Notable American Women,* ed. Edward T. James, Janet Wilson James, and Paul Boyer. Cambridge: Harvard University Press, 1971.

EDITORIAL NOTE.

In this paper Miss Fletcher has treated the subject of Indian music in a manner both novel and instructive. Her long residence among the Indians and her success in winning their love and perfect confidence have enabled her to penetrate the meaning of many things which to an ordinary observer of Indian life are incomprehensible. She is able to put herself mentally in the Indians' place and regard them and their acts from their own standpoint. It is this which gives importance to all that Miss Fletcher writes. She describes the thoughts and acts of her Indian friends as they would describe them, while her scientific training leads her to analytical work and thence to an understanding of the meaning of what she sees and hears. The present memoir is therefore to be taken as the work of one who has conscientiously studied the subject and after years of patient investigation has presented it in a form which can readily be comprehended by others. No doubt some critical student of music and of its primitive expressions will question Miss Fletcher's conclusions, particularly her method of presentation and her views upon the existence of harmony; but such criticism will be shorn of its force unless the critic has made an equally careful study of the subject among the people and can show as good reasons for a different opinion.

The technical questions involved are so well expressed and discussed by Professor Fillmore in his "report" following Miss Fletcher's paper that the whole subject is now placed fairly before students for their consideration.

On reading the manuscript of this joint work of Miss Fletcher and Mr. La Flesche and the critical analysis by Professor Fillmore, I became impressed with the scientific value of the memoir and consequently take pleasure in issuing it in the series of Museum Papers.

This publication, however, would not have been possible at present had it not been for the timely assistance of Mrs. Mary Copley Thaw who, in appreciation of Miss Fletcher and her work, has founded the fellowship which enables Miss Fletcher to devote the remainder of her life to the preparation of her Indian memoirs. For this act and example ethnologists will ever be grateful to Mrs. Thaw.

F. W. PUTNAM,

Curator of the Peabody Museum.

Cambridge, June 17, 1893.

ARCHÆOLOGICAL AND ETHNOLOGICAL PAPERS

OF THE

PEABODY MUSEUM.

— Harvard University —

VOL. I. No. 5.

A STUDY OF

OMAHA INDIAN MUSIC

BY

ALICE C. FLETCHER,

ASSISTANT IN AMERICAN ETHNOLOGY, PEABODY MUSEUM, AND
HOLDER OF THE THAW FELLOWSHIP.

AIDED BY

FRANCIS LA FLESCHE.

WITH A

REPORT ON THE

STRUCTURAL PECULIARITIES OF THE MUSIC

BY

JOHN COMFORT FILLMORE, A.M.

CAMBRIDGE, MASS.
PEABODY MUSEUM OF AMERICAN
ARCHÆOLOGY AND ETHNOLOGY.
JUNE, 1893.

A Study of Omaha Indian Music

A STUDY OF OMAHA INDIAN MUSIC.

AFTER more than ten years of constant study, during which I have had the invaluable aid of Mr. FRANCIS LA FLESCHE and the technical council and assistance of Miss SARAH ELIOT NEWMAN and Prof. JOHN COMFORT FILLMORE, I no longer hesitate to present to the public the following collection of Omaha Indian Songs, feeling confident that therein is truthfully set forth in a manner intelligible to members of my own race the Indian's mode of expressing emotion in musical forms.

I well remember my first experience in listening to Indian music. Although from habit as a student I had endeavored to divest myself of preconceived ideas, and to rise above prejudice and distaste, I found it difficult to penetrate beneath the noise and hear what the people were trying to express. I think I may safely say that I heard little or nothing of Indian music the first three or four times that I attended dances or festivals, beyond a screaming downward movement that was gashed and torn by the vehemently beaten drum. The sound was distressing, and my interest in this music was not aroused until I perceived that this distress was peculiarly my own, every one else was so enjoying himself (I was the only one of my race present) that I felt sure something was eluding my ears; it was not rational that human beings should scream for hours, looking and acting as did these Indians before me, and the sounds they made not mean something more than mere noise. I therefore began to listen below this noise, much as one must listen to the phonograph, ignoring the sound of the machinery before the registered tones of the voice are caught. I have since watched Indians laboring with a like difficulty when their songs were rendered to them upon the piano ; their ears were accustomed to the *portamento* of the voice in the song, which was broken up by the hammers of the instrument on the strings, producing such confusion of sound that it was hard for the Indians to hear and recognize the tune. My efforts in listening below the noise were rewarded by my hearing the music, and I discovered that there was in these Indian songs matter worth study and record.

My first studies were crude and full of difficulties, difficulties that I afterward learned were bred of preconceived ideas, the influence of generally accepted theories concerning "savage" music. The tones, the scales, the rhythms, the melodies that I heard, which after months of work stood out more and more clearly as indisputable facts, lay athwart these theories and could not be made to coincide with them. For a considerable time I was more inclined to distrust my ears than my theories, but when I strove to find facts that would agree with these theories I met only failure. Meanwhile the Indians sang on, and I faithfully noted their songs, studying their character and their relation to Indian life and ceremonial. During these investigations I was stricken with a severe illness and lay for months ministered to in part by Indian friends. While I was thus shut in from the rest of the world, with the Indians coming and going about me in their affectionate solicitude, they would often at my request sing for me. They sang softly because I was weak, and there was no drum, and then it was that the distraction of noise and confusion of theory were dispelled, and the sweetness, the beauty and meaning of these songs were revealed to me. As I grew stronger I was taught them, and sang them with my Indian friends, and when I was able to be carried about, my returning health was celebrated by the exemplification of the Wa-wan[1] ceremony with its music.

The ceremony took place in a large earth lodge two or three miles distant. I was laid in the bottom of a wagon and driven along the bluffs of the Missouri river, overtaking men, women and children on their ponies all headed toward the lodge, where we arrived just as the sun dropped like a red ball below the horizon. A few old men were sitting on the dome-like roof, while boys and dogs chased each other up the grassy, flowery sides of the picturesque dwelling. At the door of the long projection forming the entrance to the lodge stood friends ready to welcome me. I was lifted carefully from the wagon bed, borne by strong arms within and placed on a sort of lounge made of skins arranged nearly opposite the entrance. The people gathered by scores until between two and three hundred were seated around the central fire that leaped up brightly making

[1] The italicized *n* has a nasal sound as in the French word *en*.

the blackened roof of poles shine like polished ebony. Every one was glad and welcomed me with no uncertain word or glance. Soon I heard the cadences of the ceremonial Song of Approach. I knew the tune, I had been taught it in my sickness, and now I listened understandingly to the familiar strains as they came nearer and nearer until the bearers of the Pipes of Fellowship were seen coming down the long entrance way, waving the feather pendants of the Calumets they bore. As they turned into the lodge the whole people took up the song and I too joined, able at last to hear and comprehend the music that had through all my difficulties fascinated even while it eluded me. The occasion of this exemplification was one I can never forget, not only because of the insight it gave me into the music of the people and the meaning of the ceremony I witnessed, but because of its deeper revelation of the heart and inner life of the Indian. From that time forth I ceased to trouble about theories of scales, tones, rhythm and melody, and trusted the facts which daily accumulated in my willing hands.

I have transcribed several hundreds of Omaha songs, and have also taken down songs of the Dakotas, Otoes and Poncas, tribes belonging to the same linguistic family as the Omahas. The Pawnees are of another stock and their songs, of which I have a number, present shades of difference that may become more defined when I have worked over a larger collection of their music; the songs of the Nez Percé of Idaho also show differences that are interesting and well worth study, but these songs from different stocks have in them nothing radically divergent from the music of the Omahas, so that the facts herein set forth would seem to pertain to the music of various linguistic families.

Indian songs I have discovered travel far, and those of one tribe are soon at home in another. There seems to have been quite an extended acquaintance between tribes, the Rocky Mountains proving no serious barrier. Customs and songs borrowed from the Crow Indians have obtained for a century at least among the Nez Percé. Dakota songs are also found there with an equally remote introduction. The Omahas took from the Sioux the Ma-wa-da-ne songs, and from the Otoe, the Hae-ka-ne. The Dakotas appropriated the Omaha Hae-thu-ska songs, as did the Winnebagos. I have had Omahas sing me the songs of many different tribes, but they were always credited to the tribe to which they belonged. I have never met an instance of plagiarism among the Indians. Certain kinds

of songs can be purchased by individuals, and the song becomes
personal property, but the purchaser would never claim to have
composed it.

Professor Fillmore in his valuable report demonstrates the existence of a " natural harmonic sense " in the Indian which had been
apparent to me in my field researches.   I first detected this feeling
for harmony while rendering to the Indians their melodies upon an
instrument ; the song played as an unsupported solo did not satisfy
my memory of their unison singing, and the music did not "sound
natural" to them, but when I added a simple harmony my ear was
content and the Indians were satisfied.   What years of observations forced me to recognize, Professor Fillmore has also discovered
in his exhaustive study of the structure of these songs.   Leaving
to his scholarly treatment the technicalities of the music, I shall
restrict myself to the consideration of the relations existing between
the Indian's music and his life, social and individual.

Among the Indians, music envelopes like an atmosphere every religious, tribal and social ceremony as well as every personal experience.   There is not a phase of life that does not find expression
in song.   Religious rituals are embedded in it, the reverent recognition of the creation of the corn, of the food-giving animals, of the
powers of the air, of the fructifying sun, is passed from one generation to another in melodious measures ; song nerves the warrior
to deeds of heroism and robs death of its terrors ; it speeds the spirit
to the land of the hereafter and solaces those who live to mourn ;
children compose ditties for their games, and young men by music
give zest to their sports ; the lover sings his way to the maiden's
heart, and the old man tunefully evokes those agencies which can
avert death.   Music is also the medium through which man holds
communion with his soul, and with the unseen powers which control
his destiny.

The songs of a tribe are its heritage ; many of them have been
handed down through generations and embody not only the feeling
of the composer, but record some past event or experience ; consequently they are treasured by the people and care is taken to trans-
mit them accurately and this is effected without the usual external
aids to memory common to races who have a written language.

People who possess written music have also some mechanical

device by which a tone can be uniformly produced, as by the vibrations of a cord of given length and tension, the tone of such a cord becoming the standard by which all other tones can be regulated ; thus a succession of tones can be recorded, and accurately repeated at long intervals of time, and by different persons. The Indians have no mechanism for determining a pitch, there is no uniform key for a song, it can be started on any note suitable to the singer's voice. This absence of a standard pitch, and the Indian's management of the voice which is similar in singing and in speaking, make Indian music seem to be out of tune to our ears conventionally trained to distinguish between the singing and the speaking tone of voice. Although the Indians have no fixed pitch, yet, given a starting note, graduated intervals are observed ; not that any Indian can sing a scale, but he repeats his songs without any material variation. Men with good voices and memories are the music teachers, who take pride in their accuracy of singing, and frequently have at their command several hundred tribal songs, as the number of native songs in a tribe is always very large.

The baritone and mezzo soprano are more common than the higher or lower class of voices. The habit of singing in the open air to the accompaniment of percussion instruments tends to strain the voice to the detriment of its sweetness of tone and mobility of expression. There is little attempt on the part of the Indian singer to render *piano* or *forte* passages, or to swell and diminish a tone, although this is sometimes noticeable in love songs. When more than one person take part in a song the voices are always in unison ; the different qualities of the male and female voice bring out harmonic effects which are enhanced by the practice of the women using the falsetto ; the chord usually presents to the ear two or three octaves struck simultaneously, and one becomes aware of over tones.

The Indian enjoys the effect produced by vibrations of the voice, upon a prolonged note, he will give a throbbing tremolo not unlike the sound obtained by vibrating the string of a 'cello while passing over it the bow in an undulating movement. In the love song the singer sometimes waves his hand slowly to and from his mouth to break the flow of the breath and produce pulsations ; the tremolo of the voice does not break the tone to his ear, as do the vibrations produced by striking the piano strings. I have mentioned the difficulty which besets the Indian the first time he hears his tribal songs

played upon the piano; his trouble with the instrument has generally been removed by my singing a few bars with the piano; thus
led by the voice upon the melody, he has easily followed it to the
end. One day a Ponca who had been struggling with a piano rendering of a well-known song said:

"The Omahas and Poncas speak the same language, yet there is
something I cannot explain which makes a difference, so that we
Poncas can always tell even in the dark when it is an Omaha speaking. It is the same way with this piano and the songs, their music
is familiar, yet when you play them it is like the Omaha speaking;
when they are sung it is like the Ponca talking."

Words clearly enunciated in singing break the melody to the Indian ear and mar the music. They say of us that we "talk a great
deal as we sing." Comparatively few Indian songs are supplied
with words, and when they are so supplied, the words are frequently
taken apart or modified so as to make them more melodious; moreover, the selection of the words and their arrangement do not
always correspond to that which obtains in ordinary speech. A
majority of the songs, however, are furnished almost wholly with
syllables which are not parts or even fragments of words but
sounds that lend themselves easily to singing and are without definite meaning; yet when a composer has once set syllables to his
song, they are never changed or transposed but preserved with as
much accuracy as we would observe in maintaining the integrity of
a poem. These syllables are vowel sounds both open and nasal,
the initial letter being generally *h, th,* or *y.* While a desire for euphony directs the conscious choice of the initial letter, yet a study
of the use of these letters seems to indicate that the feeling to be
expressed controls in a measure the selection of the syllables. The
flowing *hae ha he hi ho hu* or *athae athee* lend themselves to the
gentler emotions; these sounds are common in the love-songs, the
funeral song, and when the singer breathes his desire for the
strengthening of his own life from sources beyond his sight, or
seeks to express his aspiration toward the ideal; *yah yae yee yi*
permit sharp explosive tones, and these syllables are generally employed when warlike emotions are excited.

The use of these syllables and the management of the words of
the songs reveal a striving toward poetic expression in measured
language. In order to meet the demands of the rhythm of the
music, the words of a song are frequently taken apart and melodi-

ous syllables interposed, giving to the newly formed word a measure it did not possess in ordinary speech ; accents too are changed
to meet the exigencies of rhythm, and elliptical phrases are used ;
moreover there is often an answering sound at the end of repeated
phrases made by adding a syllable ; this suggests that the expression of emotion calls for rhyme.   We seem here to come upon the
beginnings of versification, to have found the little springs of feeling and expression that lie at the source of the mighty stream of
poetry.

The following example will illustrate the foregoing :

NA-G'THE WA-AN,   Captive Song No. 1.

> Ahyae-zhum-mae *tho ;*[2]
> Ahyae-zhum-mae *tho ;*
> Ahyae-zhum-mae *tho ;*
> Hin !   We-sa-thun nu-kae-dae ;
> Ahyae-zhum-mae *tho ;*
> Ahyae-zhum-mae *tho.*

This song is sung by the leader of a war party when disaster or
death seems inevitable, and victory is to be plucked from defeat only
by the most daring and heroic efforts.   Under such circumstances,
or when death alone can be the issue of a combat, these strains are
sung to nerve the warrior to do his utmost.   The song awakens in
the memory of the soldier the joy at his birth, when his sister came
to his mother's retired tent and seeing the new-born infant, with a
cry of delight and endearment exclaimed ; "My Brother ! A man
lies there :" A man, who will ever guard from danger and hunger and
death.   The thought of that home joy and trust stimulates the
warrior beset by dangers to defy death and fulfil the prediction at
his birth.

The phrase Ahyae-zhum-mae *tho* is elliptical, made so to accord
with the rhythm of the music.   The spoken words would be Ahyae-
zhum-me ha.   In the song the phrase is oratorical, me is made
mae ; ha, denoting the close of the sentence, is changed for euphony
to the musical syllable *tho ;* the phrase as sung conveys something
more than the literal meaning of the words "they may have said ;"
"Have they not said," is the true signification ; and the ideal of a

---

[2] Throughout this monograph all italicized syllables, are not parts of words but musical syllables without definite meaning, as described in the text.

man's career is set as a gem in the words "Hi*n*! we-sa-thu*n* nu-kae-dae," My Brother! He is a man! Hi*n*, is a feminine exclamation of pleasure. We-sa-thu*n* or we-tha-thu*n*, a term of endearment used by an elder sister to her younger brother equivalent to, my dear brother. Nu-kae dae, nu, man, kae-dae, the suffix indicating the position of the infant, lying down. Through these lines twines the poetry of thought and expression, simple as a wild flower and as delicate; the music assists the tender verse and bears the weight of the thought. "Ahyae-zhum-mae *tho*" in the three musical phrases with the hold on *tho* in the third bar of each phrase, sounds the call of the man's birth prophecy, the long-echoing notes carry the thoughts over the plains and the forests that have known his footsteps, where dwell the omniscient birds that watch over the brave man, taking note of his deeds.[1] The musical treatment of these same words when they follow the fourth phrase makes them simply narrative, but in the last three bars the words become again significant, taking on a deeper meaning, one that partakes of an oracular character, as, "Have they not said, A man!" The climax of both poem and song is in this last phrase and it cannot fail to be felt by anyone following the words and music.

The Wa-oo wa-a*n* (woman songs) resemble our ballads. They are narrative and tell of happenings in the life of the composer, and, as their name implies, are experiences of young men and women. They are sung by young men when in each others' company and are seldom overheard by women, almost never by women of high character; men in mature life, unless of the old beaux class, forego these songs, as the Wa-oo wa-a*n* belong to that season in a man's career when "wild oats" are said to be sown. Many of them are quite pleasing both as to music and versification, a few are vulgar, and some are humorous.

For our understanding of these songs, a knowledge of Indian customs and modes of living is necessary, for these are all implied in the situations which give point to the ballads. To the tent or lodge come few young men except the kindred of the family, and as among the Omahas marriage in the gens of the father and subgens of the mother is forbidden, there is little chance for a girl to meet in her parents' tent a lover and be openly wooed by him. Court-

---

[1] These birds are represented in the pack used in testing a warrior's record according to the rites of the Tent of War.

ing is always in secret, the lovers usually meeting at the spring whither the girls go in the early morning and at evening for the family supply of water. The lover, however, is apt to haunt the abode of his sweetheart to watch her movements from some hidden vantage point, and at the dawn his love-song may be heard echoing over the hills. Sometimes he sings in the evening to let the maiden know of his presence. Girls find ways of learning who are the young men seeking them, and they also in their turn watch these lovers secretly and either flirt a little or entertain a serious regard for the young wooer. All this little drama takes place covertly, no elder is made a confidant; girls, however, sometimes compare notes with each other. Generally an honorable courtship ends in a more or less speedy elopement and marriage, but there are men and women who prefer dalliance, and it is this class that furnish the heroes and heroines of the Wa-oo wa-an.

In the following example, No. 2, as is commonly the case, the song is without any setting. There is no description of the heroine or of her surroundings, her lament only is given, a lament addressed to the lover who, having won her, holds so full possession of her thoughts that she has unconsciously betrayed her relation to him. The picture of the song is one common in Indian life. The twilight is deepening, the evening meal is over, the father and mother, the grandparents, the uncle, the brothers and sisters are all gathered about the cheerful fire, whose smoke curls lazily up through the opening of the tent and the children and puppies are sleepy in the quiet restfulness of the hour. The elder daughter sits demurely at the back of the tent, her fingers idling over a bit of porcupine quill embroidery she can no longer see to work upon, her thoughts are busy with the youth who has wooed her more ardently than prudence would sanction; upon this peaceful scene falls the clear voice of a singer as he passes on to the trysting place. The girl hears the well-known tones and the blood mounts to her cheek and her heart beats fast, the old men about the fire carelessly ask; "Who is that singing?" the girl in the stress of her emotion unconsciously lets slip from her lips the name of her lover. At the word all eyes turn upon her and she realizes what she has done and her confusion gives place to anger at her lack of self-control, so when she meets her lover she reproachfully tells him of her betrayal of their secret. The song is composed by the vain youth who in it rehearses his conquest to his companions.

Da-du*n* na e-bá-hu*n* beah-ke-thae, *thae*
Da-du*n* na e-ba-hu*n* beah-ke-thae, *thae*
Ha*n*-ah-de oo-tha-g'tha-ah thu*n* e-zha-zhae we-b'tha-dae thae ; *thae*
Da-du*n* na e-ba-hu*n* beah-ke-thae : *tha hi*
Ae-bae-in-tae *thae* ! ah-be-da*n* ae-hae me-kae thae ; *thae*
Wa-gu*n*-tha-ma ae-hae me-kae thae ; *thae*
E-zha-zhae we-b'tha-dae thae : *tha hi.*

Da-du*n*, an exclamation for which there is no exact English
equivalent, the word denotes trouble in the sense of a fear of con-
sequences, if one knew of a friend who was placing himself in an
equivocal relation Da-du*n* might naturally be used to express the
dread of his future shame. Na, an abbreviation of ae-na, an exclamation of surprise. In the two exclamations da-du*n* na, the
girl gives voice to her apprehension and her surprise that she should
have allowed herself to do as she did, there is also an implied
self-reproach, and a reflection upon her lover. E-ba-hu*n*, known ;
be-ah-ke-thae, I have made myself. The italicized words at the
end of the lines are musical syllables. Ha*n*-ah-de, last night ; oo-
thá-g'tha-ah, you sang, literally, shouted ; thu*n*, is a portion of the
word tae-thu*n*-de, when ; e-zha-zhae, name ; we-b'tha-dae, I spoke
your, or I called your ; thae, the feminine termination of a sentence.
Ae-bae-in-tae, who is it ; ah-be-da*n*, when they said ; ae-hae me-kae,
I said sitting ; thae, the feminine termination of the sentence. Wa-
gu*n*-tha-ma, the lover's name, the final syllable ma being a suffix
indicating that Wa-gu*n*-tha was moving, passing along ; ae-hae
me-kae, I said sitting ; thae, feminine termination of the sentence.
E-zha-zhae, name ; we-b'tha-dae, I spoke your ; thae, feminine termination of the sentence.

In ordinary speech the feminine termination of a sentence is hae,
corresponding to the masculine ha ; in oratory the men use tha, instead of ha, and women thae, rather than hae. In the poem, thae,
the formal word, is used, and tends to give dramatic feeling to the
lines. The syllables *thae tha* are added for rhythm and *hi* is used
in place of the usual *tho-e* which marks the close of the first part ;
hi is also used at the close of the last line instead of *tho*, which
generally indicates that the song is finished.

In the following translation the exclamation and syllables are
retained, as no adequate rendering of them is possible.

Da-dun'na! I have made myself known; *thae!*
Da-dun'na! I have made myself known; *thae!*
Last night when you sang, I uttered your name, *thae!*
Da-dun*n*a! I have made myself known: *tha! hi.*
"Who is it that sings?" *thae!* they said, and I sitting there, *thae!*
"Wa-gu*n*-tha is passing" I said; *thae!*
It was your name I uttered! *tha hi.*

The structure of the song reveals a groping after metrical form, and the choice of the words as well as their arrangement, which is not colloquial, indicates a desire to express the story effectively and to lift it above the commonplace. The use of the syllable *thae* as a musical refrain at the end of each line is noteworthy. The introduction of *thae* in the fifth line after Ae-bae-in-tae, "Who is it that sings?" has the effect of a sigh, adding dramatic expression and a touch of pathos to the narrative. The opening lines presenting at once the theme of the song, resemble in a striking manner the chorus of a Scotch ballad that always sets forth the central thought or feeling, around which all the circumstances of the story cluster. In the Indian song, however, there is no elaboration in literary form, and the music is equally simple; the thought, the scene, the melody, come without warning or prelude, breathe out their burden and are gone almost before a listener of our own race realizes their presence.

Examples of nascent poetry could be multiplied, were further illustration necessary, to show that the Omahas had begun to use simple metrical forms. Their oratory and many of their ordinary figures of speech afford abundant proof of their poetic feeling; in their songs we see indications that the demand of the rhythm of emotion for an answering expression in measured language was more or less consciously recognized, but we fail to find evidence of the sustained intellectual effort essential to the development of poetic art.

The following collection shows how pervasive were the Omaha songs not only in the social and political forms of the tribe but in permeating the avocations of the people, and the beliefs and aspirations of the individual Indian.

The songs fall into three groups:

   I.   CLASS SONGS.
  II.   SOCIAL SONGS.
 III.   INDIVIDUAL SONGS.

The first group embraces the songs of the Sacred Pole, and Buffalo Hide ; the Hae-de-wa-che or annual tribal dance : those pertaining to the rites of the Tent of War ; and the ritual of the filling of the Tribal Pipes.   These songs are either religious or ritualistic and are sung only by the initiated, or by the members of certain subgentes having charge of sacred or of tribal ceremonies.

The second group includes songs belonging to the Poo-g'thun, Hae-thu-ska, To-ka-lo, Ma-wa-da-ne, and other secular or secret societies ; also all dance and game songs ; the songs of the Wa-wan or ceremony of the Pipes of Fellowship ; and the Funeral song. These songs are always sung by companies of persons ; the last two are somewhat religious in character, but are not sacerdotal.

To the third group belong the In-g'thunwa-an (Thunder songs), and those which relate to Mystery, to Dreams, and to the Sweat Lodge ; Na-g'the wa-an (Captive or Death songs) ; Mekasee (Wolf or Brave songs) ; Wae-ton wa-an (Woman's songs of Sorrow) ; Love lays ; Songs of Thanks, and the Prayer taught every Omaha child by its parents and used throughout life by the whole tribe. These songs pertain to individual hopes, desires, or experiences and they are generally sung as solos.

I. CLASS SONGS.

SONGS OF THE SACRED POLE AND THE BUFFALO HIDE.

The Omaha tribe lived in the buffalo country, and their hunting of this game was governed by well defined rules and regulations which were obligatory upon every member of the tribe, were rigorously enforced, and any disobedience was severely punished by officers appointed to execute the laws.   Early in July the entire tribe moved out of their village under a leader who had been ceremoniously placed in command.   Upon this man rested the sole responsibility of directing the movements of the tribe, of selecting their camping places, of searching for the game, and of regulating the manner of hunting and securing food.   He was held accountable for everything that happened, for the attacks of enemies without, and for quarrels within, even down to the fighting of the dogs.   If disasters occurred the leader was deposed, for it was considered that his prayers were ineffectual, and he was not in favor with the Unseen Powers.   The tribe, when moving, kept well together and often stretched out a mile or two in length, and was guarded by picked men detailed from the bravest of the warriors ; this soldier police force not only looked out for lurking enemies, but prevented any man slipping from the ranks for a private hunt. All the rules respecting the movements of the tribe on the annual hunt were based upon the principle that the liberty of the individual must be subordinated to the welfare of the community, and therefore no one for his personal pleasure or gain was permitted to infringe any of the time-honored regulations. The Leader traveled apart at one side, in prayerful contemplation of the duties which devolved upon him. His office was one of the most coveted within the tribal gift and was also one of the most onerous.

After the tribe had secured an ample store of meat, sufficient to meet the requirements of the winter season, the festival of Thanksgiving took place ; on this occasion the Sacred Pole and the Buffalo Hide were taken from their tents and became the central objects in the ceremony. The Wa-hrae'-hae-ta*n*, a sub-gens of the Hu*n*ga gens, had charge of the Pole and its tent and the Wa-sha-ba-ta*n* another subgens cared for the Hide and its tent. To the Hu*n*ga was entrusted the preservation of the ritual and songs of the Pole, and no one in the tribe except a male member of this gens had the right to sing these hubae wa-a*n* or sacred songs.[1]

Song No. 3 was sung when the ceremony of anointing the Pole was about to take place, and was a call to the people to gather together to witness the rite.   Some of the words are evidently modified so as to be more musical, as in the first line where Ae-hae when repeated is changed to thae-hae; "Ae-hae thae-hae" being more euphonious and flowing than ae-hae ae-hae.

Ae-hae thae-hae *tha*
Ae-gu*n* shu-ka-tha-ha nuz-zhi*n*-ga
Ae-hae thae-hae *tha*
Mu*n*-da-ha ae-ah ba-da*n* ae-ah
Ae-hae thae-hae *tha.*

Ae-hae, I bid or command ; Ae-gu*n*, therefore ; shu-ka-tha-ha, in a group ; nuz-zhi*n*-ga, stand ye ; Mu*n*-da-ha is an obsolete word, as is ae-ah, the meaning however seems to be, gather, come nearer ; ba-da*n*, and ; the word ae-gu*n* is difficult to translate, it implies that the Hu*n*ga having been formally requested by the chiefs to perform this ceremony ae-gu*n* (therefore) the people on their part are to gather and stand near the sacred tent and witness it.

[1] A full account of the Pole or Wa-hrae'-hae and the ceremonies connected with it, and all other rites pertaining to the tribe will be given in a monograph entitled " The Omahas."

> I bid I bid *tha*
> Therefore, shall ye all stand in a group
> I bid I bid *tha*
> Gather ye nearer, come hither, come !
> I bid I bid *tha*.

The following song, No. 4, was sung during the painting of the Sacred Pole.

> Zhe-da ke-thae zhe-da ke-thae *hae hae*
> Kum-peah ke-thae kum-peah ke-thae *hae hae*

Zhe-da, red ; ke-thae, I make ; kum-peah, comely, pleasant to look upon.

> I make the Pole red and comely to look upon.

There are a number of ritual songs belonging to this ceremony which tell of the creation and growth of the corn; the music of these, like the foregoing example, is of the chant order.

On the third day of the Thanksgiving festival the Hae-de-wa-che or tribal dance took place conducted by the In-kae-sabbae gens ; the singing of the songs was the duty of the Wa-the-ge-zhae subgens. The dance was highly dramatic especially that part wherein the past experiences of the warriors were depicted. The scene was full of action and color, the whole tribe took part in it ; every one was in gala dress, there was hardly an Omaha too old or too young not to have upon him some token of festivity. Fragments of ancient tribal rites are discernible in this dance, as well as bits of tribal history ; the music however presents little of interest it being simple in rhythm, and fitted to the movements of the dancing men and women as they pass in a vast circle around a pole,[1] the male singers and drummers sitting at its base.

The Call to the Hae-de-wa-che No. 5 is peculiar and noteworthy. Its melodious cadences suggest the echo of some well nigh forgotten song which belonged possibly to an obsolete rite that has long since been lost or merged in this dance of the tribe.

> Zha-wa e-ba e-ba *ha*
> Ae-hae

are the words. Zha-wa is an abridgment of oo-zha-wa, to rejoice ; eba, come ; ae-hae, I command.

---

[1] The pole used in the Hae-de-wa-che is not the Sacred Pole, but one cut for the occasion with peculiar ceremonies.

Come! Come and rejoice!
I bid you!

The words in the dance song, No. 6, are, Ae-hae wa-na-shae, I command, soldiers. The bidding was from the In-kae-sabbae gens to the soldiers of the tribe to take part in the dance.

SONGS OF THE TENT OF WAR.

The Wae-jin-ste gens had charge of the Tent of War wherein were preserved certain articles used in those rites which were supposed to test the truthfulness of a warrior's recital of his deeds of valor. One of these articles was a skin case or pack fashioned in the symbolic form of a bird and containing the skins of a number of birds supposed to possess warlike instincts. These birds in their flight over the earth watched and noted all valorous deeds, so when a man boasted or exaggerated as he told his tale in the presence of this pack, his untruthfulness was brought to light by these birds who caused the reed which he was required to drop upon the pack to roll off to the ground. The rites of the Tent of War are allied to those ceremonies connected with the hearing of the first thunder peal in the spring-time. There are indications of a kinship of ideas and emotions between the songs of the War-Tent ceremony and the Ing'than wa-an (thunder songs) :[1] the latter, being the expression of an individual appeal to the unseen powers, are more varied and tuneful; the former, belonging to a ceremonial are, of necessity restricted and formal, resembling a chant rather than a melody. These differences, however, do not conceal the likeness between the two classes of songs, and there is reason to believe that the resemblance has an historical basis, and that the chants of the Tent of War were once Thunder songs of individuals which became in the lapse of years modified to suit the ritual as sung during the truth-testing rites of the Tent of War.

The following No. 7 is an example of the songs pertaining to these rites. The words refer to the mythical form and weapon of Thunder.

The-te-gan num-pae-wa-thae! *ga*.
The-te-gan num-pae-wa-thae! *ga*
The-te-gan num-pae-wa-thae! *ga*
The-te-gan wae-tin kae g'the-hun ke num-pae-wa-thae! *ga*
The-te-gan num-pae-wa-thae! *ga*.

---

[1] These songs are Nos. 75, 76, 77.

The-te-ga*n*, your grandfather; num-pae-wa-thae, fearful to be-hold; wae-ti*n*, club; kae, long; g'the-hu*n*, lifts his; ke, when.

> Your Grandfather fearful to behold is he! *ga*
> Your Grandfather fearful to behold is he! *ga*
> Your Grandfather fearful to behold is he! *ga*
> When your Grandfather lifts his long club he is fearful to behold! *ga*
> Your Grandfather fearful to behold is he! *ga*

It is only in rituals, or the songs of a religious ceremony that there is ever any picturing of the gods, any attempt to appeal to the imagination and stir the emotions of awe or fear. In this song not only is Thunder addressed, but his powerful ancestors are called to mind. Myths tell of these wonderful beings who some-times descended to avenge wrong doing and this song recalls a time when Thunder warred against man.

The music of the ritual of filling the Tribal Pipes is lost. The keeping of this ritual was the hereditary charge of certain members of a subgens of the In-shtae-sunda gens, and the last man who knew it died some years ago. It was a chant and was sung without accentuation by the drum.

All the songs of group I are Hubae wa-a*n*, sacred songs and were the property of certain subgentes and initiated persons. Although many of these songs, as those of the Hae-de wa-che, and the Sacred Pole were often learned stealthily by ear, no persuasion could in-duce a man not of the In-kae-sabbae or Hu*n*ga gens to sing them in the presence of a member of either of these gentes; it would be as-suming a right or tribal privilege, and as unbecoming an Omaha, as for an obscure person among us to arrogate to himself the func-tions of an official. It is difficultt to obtain a hearing of these songs apart from their appropriate ceremonies; those here given have been obtained through personal friendship of the singers.

II. SOCIAL SONGS.

Societies afforded the only opportunities within the tribe for the indulgence of the social instinct, membership not being confined to any one gens; persons who were not kindred could thus meet upon terms of equality. The various gatherings were occasions for the display of talent and the enjoyment of applause or the practice of rites supernatural in their import. Some of the societies bore a resemblance to our clubs, others were historical, religious or secret.

These associations embraced within their membership almost every adult man and many women in the tribe.

POO-G'THUN SONGS.

The Poo-g'thun society is said to be one of the oldest. Chiefs only were eligible and a candidate once admitted remained a member until death. The Leader or principal officer was that chief who could count the greatest number of valiant deeds, therefore unless a man kept up his war record he could hardly hope to retain this position. The office of Keeper of the songs was held for life and it was the duty of the incumbent to train his successor. The songs were the archives of the society; little more than the name of a noted chief might be mentioned in the song but the story of the hero's deeds was stored in the Keeper's memory and transmitted with the song, thus the traditions of the Poo-g'thun preserved a partial history of the tribe. Through a series of coincidences a superstition grew up that whenever the Keeper sang one of the old songs death would visit his family; members therefore became loath to take the responsibility of asking for them, and when the request was made it was accompanied by a large gift, offered to atone for any ill fortune which might come upon the Keeper. It is said that the last time the Keeper sang an old song, while he was singing, a Sioux warrior crept stealthily into the camp, made his way to the singer's tent and there shot dead the Keeper's daughter. The society has been extinct for about half a century and the stories connected with the Poo-g'thun Songs are lost; no one knows by whom they were composed or the events they celebrate. The songs are of two kinds : those sung while the men sat resting, and those which served as an accompaniment to dancing.[1]

In Song No. 8, musical syllables are used in all the phrases except in that at the commencement of the second part. En-da-koo-tha, an old word for friend; wa-ha-tun-ga, shield; ae-ah-mae, they say. Wa-ha-tunga was probably the hero's name, and the song may record this man's services as a friend to the people, or as a shield. The song is lively, easily starts the heels, and once heard is not apt to be forgotten; the music has by these qualities outlived its burden.

---

[1] A full account of the Societies of the Omahas will be given in the Omaha monograph.

The words of No. 9 are also few and the hero whose war cry is recorded is now forgotten.

Shu-pe-da hu-ah-ta na-zhin; *thae,*
Shu-pe-da hu-ah-ta na-zhin; *thae,*
Ah ae thae tha!
Ae thae he thae!
Ae-hae hu-ah-ta na-zhin; *thae,*
Ae thae tha!
Ae thae he thae!

Shu-pe-da, when I come; hu-ah-ta, I shout, I cry; na-zhin, stand. These scanty words convey to the Omaha the picture of the warrior who, when he reaches his place in the battle line, shouts forth his cry that sends terror to the enemy.

When I come to my place I shout; *thae,*
When I come to my place I shout; *thae,*
Ah ae thae tha!
Ae thae he thae!
I command as I stand and shout; *thae,*
Ae thae tha!
Ae thae he thae!

The following, No. 10, is full of spirit and defiance, a real war-song.

Shu-pe-da wea-wa-ta tha-wa-thae
Shu-pe-da wea-wa-ta tha-wa-thae
Pa-tha-ga-ta!
Tha wa thae *ah hae thae he*
Thae ah he thae!

Shu-pe-da, when I come; wea-wa-ta, where; tha-wa-thae, do I send them; Pa-tha-ga-ta, to the hill or mounds.[1]

Where do I send them when I come?
Where do I send them when I come?
To their graves!
I send them *ah hae thae he*
Thae ah he thae!

A song so full of bravery could not die in the memory of a people as valiant as the Omahas.

The war-cry at the close of these songs is not vociferous, but seems to be addressed to that particular guardian of the warrior which

[1] The Omahas erected mounds over their dead.

had appeared to him in his fastings and whose token was always worn on his person in the hour of danger. Such cries possessed a subjective character, they roused within the singer the memory of his vigils when the promise of supernatural help in time of need was given, they nerved him to greater power, while they reminded his enemy that he had to contend with an unseen ally in the battle ; they were altogether different from the yell or whoop so generally present in Indian warfare, and were used for a very different purpose.

The Poo-g'thun wa-an constitute the wildest music of the Omahas and, unlike other war-songs of the tribe, they are marked by a rhythm, simple and forceful, and are quite in contrast with many of the Hae-thu-ska songs wherein the rhythms are contesting and complicated.

HAE-THU-SKA SONGS.

The origin of the Hae-thu-ska society is not known, there is a tradition that it sprang from the Poo-g'thun and there are reasons which give weight to this view. A valiant record alone entitled a man to admission and promotion in the Hae-thu-ska ; a chief secured no precedence, for the society was democratic as to the standing of its members. Like the Poo-g'thun, the Hae-thu-ska preserved the history of its members in its songs ; when a brave deed was performed, the society decided whether it should be celebrated and without this dictate no man would dare permit a song to be composed in his honor. When a favorable decision was given, the task of composing the song devolved upon some man with musical talent. It has happened that the name of a man long dead has given place in a popular song to that of a modern warrior ; this could only be done by the consent of the society, which was seldom given as the Omahas were averse to letting the memory of a brave man die. There are a few songs that carry two names, the old being still remembered, although a new name is gradually taking its place. This overlapping offers a clew as to the age of the song, since a man's name would not be dropped during the life time of any near kindred ; it seems safe to date such songs fully fifty years prior to the substitution of the new name. Although the Haethuska had no office of "Keeper of the songs," the songs were transmitted from one generation to another with care as was also the story of the deeds the songs commemorated. The singing was by selected members assisted by a few women, who sat around the drum ; some of the songs were sung by the whole assembly, particularly those used in the opening and closing ceremonies.

The officers of the Hae-thu-ska comprised a Leader, a Herald and two Servers who held their places for life, or until they resigned. The meetings of the Society generally took place once a month, but there were no stated times. The Herald, on the evening of a meeting, four times sounded the call "Hae-thu-ska !" prolonging the last syllable which echoed among the hills and woods, producing an effect not unlike soft modulating chords. The first act after the members were gathered together was the preparation of the charcoal for blackening the face in honor of Thunder. Song No. 11 was sung as the box elder wood charred upon the fire.

> Nun-g'thae thae-tae
> He-tha-ke-un-tae
> Thun-ah-he-dae.

Nun-g'thæ, charcoal ; thæ-tae, this standing before me. He-tha-ke-un-tae, to paint or decorate himself with ; thun-ah-he-dae from un-tha-he-dae, I wearily wait or wait until I am weary. The song implies that the warrior is weary waiting for the time when he shall go forth to fight under the shadow or protection of Thunder, the god of War. The music expresses the eagerness of the warrior and suggests the tremulous movement of the leaves just before a thunder storm.

After the painting of the face the pipe was filled and then presented to the zenith and the four points of the compass as the assembly joined in the following prayer No. 12 :

> Wa-kan-da tha-ne ga thae kae.
> Wa-kan-da tha-ne ga thae kae.
> Wa-kan-da tha-ne ga thae kae
> Ae-ha tha-ne hin-ga
> *Wae tho hae tho*

Wa-kan-da, God ; tha-ne from ne-ne, tobacco ; ga, here ; thae, this ; kae, long ; ae-ha, now ; hin-ga, from in-ga, to draw with the lips. Wa-kan-da, we offer tobacco in this pipe, will you accept our offering and smoke it? is the meaning of the words. This prayer concluded the opening ceremonies.

The evening was spent in social converse, interspersed with

songs sung as the members sat at rest; dance songs were struck up
occasionally, each dancer acting out his personal experiences, or
the story of the song that was being sung. When a name occurred
in a song the drum ceased and the voices alone carried the music.
Food was always prepared in the presence of the assembly; when
it was ready to be served No. 13 was sung, while the servers performed a dance peculiar to this part of the evening's ceremony.

> Ou-han thae-tae ne-dae *tho.*
> En-da-koo-tha ne-dae tho.

Ou-han, cooked food, or the one who cooks the food for a company; thae-tae, this; ne-dae, it is cooked. En-da-koo-tha, the
same old word for friend as that used in the Porg'thun song No. 8;
tho, a substitute for the oratorical tha, to mark the close of the
sentence. The words proclaim, Friend, the food is cooked.

After supper, dance and resting songs were sung, dramatic
dances accompanying the former. Well on in the night, the ceremonies were brought to a close by the entire company singing the
song of dismissal No. 14. With the beginning of the song the
members arose, and, at the second part they moved slowly around
the fire singing as they walked; the thud of the feet answered to
the drum as the warriors passed out into the night, and the final
note was struck as the last man emerged from the lodge. The
meetings of the Hae-thu-ska opened and closed with chorals of a
religious character; in these ceremonial songs, as well as in other
music pertaining to War, we see how closely allied were War and
religious ceremonies among the Omahas. The music of No. 14 is
worthy of note; so is the harmony insisted upon by the Indians as
necessary to the expression of the feeling of the song when it is
rendered upon the piano. The words, though simple, show why the
Omahas demanded fuller chords for the march of the warriors around
the lodge than for the call to rise and stand, preparatory to moving
out under the stars.

> Hin-da-koo-tha na-zhin *thae.*
> Hin-da-koo-tha na-zhin *thae.*
> Hin-da-koo-tha na-zhin *thae.*
> Ae-ha na-zhin he-tha-mae *tho hae thae.*
> Hin-da-koo-tha ma-thin *thae.* etc.

Hin-da-koo-tha is the same old word used in the ceremonial song
No. 13, the letter *h* is prefixed to give musical effect and an added

meaning to the word En-da-koo-tha; the members of the Hae-thu-ska were friends bound together by experiences and deeds that had proved each one's valor and dependence upon the unseen powers, those forces that help and protect man in the hour of danger, the word recognizes this tie: na-zhin, stand; ae-ha, now; he-tha-mae, they say, they will. In the second part the only change is the substitution of ma-thin, to walk, for the word na-zhin, to stand.

Song No. 15.

> Zhin-thae sha-e-be-thae
> Zhin-thae sha-e-be-thae
> Nun-dae wae-ga-thun-ga ta-ba-dan
> Zhin-thae sha-e-be-thae *tho hae tho-e*
> Ta-hae-zhin-ga Hae-thu-ska ga-hae-dan.
> Nun-dae wae-ga-thun-ga ta-ba-dan.
> Zhin-thae sha-e-be-thae *tho hae tho.*

Zhin-thae, elder brother; Sha-e-be-thae, and Sha-e-ba-dan are modifications of Sha-e-eha, they are coming; Nun-dae, heart; wae-ga-thun-ga, to test our; ta-ba-dan, that they may; ga-hae-dan, when he made. The song may be translated:

When Ta-hae-zhin-ga was the Leader of the Hae-thu-ska he made this saying:—Brother, they are coming to test our hearts or courage.

The song is very old. The most aged men to be found in the tribe ten years ago, had heard it when they were boys sung by old warriors. The name in the text was being supplanted three generations ago by that of Ne-koo-the-b'than, and still later, Han-dan-ma-thin, who fought valiantly against the Pawnees over fifty years since, was honored by having his name occasionally introduced in the song.

Song No. 16.

> Hae-thu-ska thin-ga-bae
> Hae-thu-ska thin-ga-bae
> Hae-thu-ska thin-ga-bae
> Gha-gae ah-thin-hae *tho hae tho-e*
> Te-thu the-shan thin-ga-bae
> Hae-thu-ska thin-ga-bae
> Gha-gae ah-thin-hae *tho hae tho.*

Hae-thu-ska, the members of the Hae-thu-ska Society; thin-ga-bae, they are naught, or, they are dead; Gha-gae, I weep; ah-thin-hae, I walk; Te-thu, the village; the-shan, around.

This old song was composed at a time when so many of the
Omaha warriors had been slain that the Hae-thu-ska Society ad-
journed its meetings until the period of mourning was over; when
the members came together again, this song was sung in memory of
the days when men went about the village weeping for the brave
comrades who had fallen in battle and were seen no more.   I have
heard old men sing this song in a low tone as they sat by the fire,
tears in their faded eyes, their thoughts upon the friends who had
gone, and the days that could never return.   The double drum
beats are not here represented because to our ear they would detract
from the feeling expressed in the music, and prevent an understanding of the pathos of the song.   The thirty-second notes as rendered
by the Indian suggest the catching of the breath in sobs.
   Song No. 17.

> Tun-gae-ah da-dun nan-tha-pae he we-tha ga
> Tun-gae-ah da-dun nan-tha-pae he-we-tha ga
> Tun-gae-ah um-ba ya-dun he-we-tha ga
> Tun-gae-ah da-dun nan-tha-pae he-we-tha ga
> Tun-gae-ah um-ba ya-dan he-we-tha ga.

   Tun-gae, my sister; ah, calls the attention of the one addressed;
da-dun, what; nan-tha-pae, fear you; he-we-tha ga, tell me; um-ba,
day; ya-dan, coming.
   My sister! tell me what it is you fear as the day dawns?
   The song is old.   It was sung slowly while the members sat at
rest in the meetings of the Hae-thu-ska, and it was also one of the
songs sung as the men went out to fight.   "Sister" personates the
women of the tribe.   "What can they fear when the warriors are
gathered for their protection."   The song is knightly in its sentiment.
   Song No. 18.

> Um-ba thae-na un-ge-tun-ba ga
> Um-ba thae-na un-ge-tun-ba-gae Tun-gae
> Um-ba thae-na un-ge-tun-ba-gae *tho hae*
>   Hae-thu-ska na tae-he-ae-dae
>   Pa-hae-tae ah-ke-he-b'tha
> Um-ba thae-na un-ge-tun-ba gae *tho hae tho.*

   Um-ba, day; thae-na, this only; un-ge-tun-ba ga, look at me
who belong to you, tun is from dun-bae, to see, ge gives the pos-
sessive, ga the imperative; tun-gae, sister; hae-thu-ska, the so-

ciety membership; na, only; tae-he-ae-dae, a difficult task or duty which one is under obligation to perform; pa-hae-tae, I make myself, that is I become a part of the Hae-thu-ska society, an elliptical and poetic form. Ah-ke-he-b'tha, I feel unqualified, that is, the duty is difficult and although I shall attempt it I feel my disqualifications. "Sister look upon me who belong to you for the last time to-day, the tasks of a member of the Hae-thu-ska are difficult. I feel my shortcomings, and go forth for the last time to-day."

The song was sung when the members were resting, or when the Hae-thu-ska, circling the camp, were going forth to battle.   Sister personifies the women of the tribe.

An occasion is remembered when, over seventy-five years ago, this song was sung in a fight with the Cheyenne and Arrapahos, the Omaha camp was threatened, and many women saw their warriors for the last time as they moved off to do battle for the preservation of their homes.

Song No. 19.

> Sha-e-ba-dan wa-dan-ba ga
> Sha-e-ba-dan wa-dan-ba ga
> Sha-e-ba-dan wa-dan-ba ga
> Hae-thu-ska wa-shu-shae *tho hae thoe*
> Mun-chu-tun-ga wa-dan-ba ga
> Sha-e-ba-dan wa-dan-ba ga
> Sha-e-ba-dan wa-dan-ba ga
> Hae-thu-ska wa-shu-shae *tho hae tho.*

Sha-e-ba-dan, they are coming; wa-dan-ba ga, see them, the syllable ga indicates a command; Wa-shu-shae, warriors or braves; Mun-chu-tun-ga, the name of the man celebrated in the song.

> See them ! they are coming,
> Warriors of the Hae-thuska.
> Mun-chu-tun-ga ! behold them
> See them ! they are coming,
> Warriors of the Hae-thu-ska.

The mention of Mun-chu-tun-ga by name, when all the warriors of the Hae-thu-ska were addressed collectively, commemorated the bravery of this one man in the face of an advancing enemy.

Song No. 20.

Ho eya ae ho wae Ho e ya ae ho wae, etc.

Zhin-ga-wa-shu-shae we-gee-the-thae dan wa-nun-hae

Man-b'thin-ah tho shu-b'thae-ah thin-ha.

The first lines are syllables having no definite meaning except as the music gives them expression. Zhin-ga-wa-shu-shae, the name of the hero of the song who fell in battle; we-gee-the-thae dan, when I remember you; wa-nun-hae, spirit; Man-b'thin-ah, I walk; shu-b'thae, I am coming; ah-thin-hae, I walk.

The words are modified and fitted to the rhythm of the song and are used figuratively rather than literally. The song interpreted is Zhin-ga-wa-shu-shae, when I remember you I walk as a spirit, I am coming to become such; meaning that to avenge the killing of Zhin-ga-wa-shu-shae death must be faced, and he who avenges may lose his life; but that will not deter the warrior who declares to his friend "I am coming."

This old song was used to commemorate a battle with the Sioux some fifty years ago, and Nan-kae-nae, the name of a warrior who then fell was substituted, his mounded grave is upon the bluffs of the Missouri and beside that grave I first heard this song.

Song No. 21.

Han-thin-gae ae-ah-ma,

Han-thin-gae ae-ah-ma,

Han-thin-gae ae-ah-ma,

Wa-kan-da thin-gae ae-ah-ma,

Han-thin-ga *wae tho hae tho-e*

Han-thin-gae ae-ah-ma

Wa-kan-da thin-gae ae-ah-ma

Han-thin-ga *wae tho hae tho.*

An-thin-gae, I have nothing, literally, and so used in ordinary speech; the word in the song, however, is figurative, I become as nothing, vanish, die; in the prefixing of *H* is an attempt to express the feeling of self abnegation in the contemplation of death; ae-ah-ma, they say; Wakanda, the god or gods; thin-gae, nothing, has the same meaning as an-thin-gae, the first syllable is omitted on account of the measure of the line. The accents of the words are also modified to suit the rhythm and Han-thin-gae is changed to Han-thin-ga before the syllable *wae* for greater euphony. These words, if spoken colloquially in the order here given, would be without meaning; but, as used in the song, in a figurative and elliptical sense, they become highly poetic, and take possession of the mind. Their meaning is, the lives of men are at the command or in the keeping of the gods, when they speak, or decree, man obeys or yields up his life. The song is highly esteemed in the Omaha tribe, as expressing religious emotion, and its cadences are heard when serious thoughts come to the old or to the man in danger. I have been unable to ascertain its age, but it was known in the early part of this century, and probably was handed down from the last.

This song was sung by the members of the Hae-thu-ska when sitting at rest .

Song No. 22.

> Ah-ta*n* ta*n*-bae da*n* shae-ga*n* ah-thi*n*-hae no
> Ah-ta*n* ta*n*-bae da*n* shae-ga*n* ah-thi*n*-hae no
> Ah-ta*n* ta*n*-bae da*n* shae-ga*n* ah-thi*n*-hae no
> Gha-gae-wa-thae wa-oo hae-the-ga*n*-ae
> Ah-ta*n* ta*n*-bae da*n* shae-ga*n* ah-thi*n*-hae no
> Ah-ta*n* ta*n*-bae da*n* shae-ga*n* ah-thi*n*-bae no.

Ah-ta*n* ta*n*-bae da*n*, when I see; shae-ga*n*, likewise; ah-thi*n*-hae, I am; no, end of sentence and used instead of the ordinary word ha; Gha-gae-wa-thae, name of the man whose lack of fighting ability is signalized in the song; wa-oo, woman; hae-the-ga*n*-ae, like you. The song is old and refers to the conduct of a man who left his wounded comrade on the field to fall into the hands of the enemy, whereas a brave warrior would have stood beside his fallen friend and fought until death or victory came. The words of the song are scant and used elliptically; the meaning is, "when in a conflict, do I act like you, Gha-gae-wa-thae, you fled as a woman might have done."

Song No. 23.

> Ah-thu-ha u*n*-dum-ba-ga
> U*n*-dum-ba-ga u*n*-dum-ba-ga
> Ah-thu-ha u*n*-dum-ba-gae *tho hae*
> Ah-thu-ha u*n*-dum-ba-gae *tho hae*
> Um-ba e-da*n* hoo-ma-thu*n*
> We-ae-b'thi*n* ae-dae u*n*-dum-ba-ga
> Ah-thu-ha u*n*-dum-ba-gae *tho hae*
> Ah-thu-ha u*n*-dum-ba-gae *tho hae*

Ah-thu-ha, again; un-dum-ba-ga or Um-ba e-dan, in the coming day, or at day dawn, see me; hoo-ma-thin they who howl. The song refers to the wolf, and the warrior here personifies himself as that animal and bids the people behold him who, as a wolf, is seeking his prey in the morning.

The song was composed by a member of the In-shta-sunda gens, a brave man, who was frequently called upon to act as a soldier guard to maintain order when the people were on the hunt; he would then ride singing; "Once again you shall use your weapons upon me," referring to the liabilities incurred in the performance of the duties imposed upon him as a guard. He is said to have shaved his hair close to his head on these occasions, painted his scalp red, and that when struck by any resisting hunter no blood flowed from the wound.

Song No. 24.

Ne-ka we-ta wa-gan-tha te-bae-no
Ne-ka we-ta wa-gan-tha te-bae-no: 11:
Nu-dan-hun-ga Ish-e-buz-zhe tha-da-e thin-kae-dae.
Ne-ka we-ta wa-gan-tha te-bae-no :11:

Ne-ka is part of the word ne-ka-she-ga, persons or people; we-ta, part of we-we-ta, my; wa-gan-tha, they want; te-bae-no, part of ah-te be-ah-no, they come; Nu-dan-hun-ga, Leader; tha-da-e, they call; thin-kae describes Ish-e-buz-zhe as sitting; dae, part of ae-ae-dae, he is the one. The song refers to the people calling for their noted Leader Ish-e-buz-zhe who remained sitting in his tent, when the enemy was approaching the camp. The song is one of the oldest known and a great favorite, not only for dancing, but because of the fame of Ish-e-buz-zhe, who lived several generations ago; his eccentricities form part of the nursery lore of the tribe, so to speak, and men tell of his queer humorous ways, his valor when once aroused, and his great physical power. A very old man who died in 1884, a member of the Tae-thin-dae gens and therefore a descendant of Ish-e-buz-zhe, said that his grandfather's grandfather when he was young saw Ish-e-buz-zhe. This throws the song back over one hundred and fifty years, at the lowest computation; the man who died in 1884 was born near the beginning of this century. His statement was confirmed by another very old man of the same gens.

TO-KA-LO SONGS.

The To-ka-lo society has been extinct for many years. It was for a time in great repute with the warriors; its dances somewhat resembled those of the Hae-thu-ska. One of the chief features of this society was its procession about the tribal circle, when all the members were dressed in full regalia and rode their best horses which were elaborately decorated. Song No. 25 was sung on their last parade as they moved slowly on their curveting steeds, to the delight of all the boys in the camp; many of these, to-day mature men, recall the scene with youthful enthusiasm. The music is well suited to the prancing step of a spirited charger. Very few songs survive from this society.

Secret societies had their songs. A few of these and all of the Ma-wa-da-ne songs were borrowed from other tribes.

IN-OU-TIN OR GAME SONGS.

Game songs are sung by young men when they gamble with sticks, pebbles, or moccasins either for fun or in earnest. Nos. 26, 27, 28 and 29 afford a fair representation of these pretty and spirited tunes which are repeated *ad libitum*, much as we use the jig and dance tunes. Words are seldom employed: there are, however, exceptions. No. 26 is an instance. E-ae zhinga, little stone; da-dan ska-hae, what are you making? refers to the tiny pebble which is being dexterously tossed from one hand to the other, the arms keeping the rhythm of the song; at its end the closed hands are stretched out for persons to guess in which one is the stone and so win or lose a stake. The grace and precision of movement together with the liveliness of the music is often very pleasing.

The alternate rhythms in song No. 27 are marked by the changing movements of those playing the game.

In the song of success No. 29, the singer humorously asks, as he gathers in the stakes he has won, "Friends! Why is it you say I am little?"

Children have songs of their own handed on from older sets of playmates to the younger coming after them; they are sung during games such as "Follow my Leader" (No. 30) when the little ones trot along keeping time to the tune.

The Omahas have few songs of their own composition that are used simply for social dancing. The Hae-kar-nee of the Otoe are favorites for this purpose. The following is an example (No. 31).

THE WA-WAN.

Wa-wan means to sing for some one and is the name given to the ceremony connected with the Pipes of Fellowship,—songs form so important a part of the ritual that the peculiar pipes used in this ceremony are called Ne-ne-ba wae-ah-wan, pipes to sing with. The songs are accompanied by rhythmic movements of the Pipe Bearers, and also of the Pipes, which are swayed to the music. These motions are termed Ne-ne-ba ba-zhan, shaking the Wa-wan pipes. As the rhythmic movements of the Pipes and their Bearers have always attracted the attention of white observers, the ceremony has been characterized by them as a "Pipe-dance" or "Calumet dance," whereas the performance does not convey to the Omaha mind the idea of a dance, nor do the movements really resemble Indian dancing, with the possible exception of that part of the ceremony which takes place on the fourth night.

The ceremony of the Wa-wan consists of the formal presentation of the Wa-wan pipes by a man of one gens to a man of another gens, or a man of one tribe to one of another. By means of this ceremony the two men become bound by a tie equal in strength and obligation to that between father and son. The man who presents the Pipes is called Wa-wan ah-ka, the one who sings; the man who receives them is spoken of as Ah-wan e-ah-ka, the one who is sung to. The Wa-wan ah-ka must be of good standing in his tribe as must also be the recipient of the Pipes; otherwise the chiefs would refuse to permit the Wa-wan to take place, and their consent is requisite to the inauguration of the ceremony.

As a considerable expenditure of property is necessary for the presenting and receiving of the Pipes, a man undertaking the ceremony mentions his plan to his kindred who contribute toward the Hun-ga wa-in, or gifts which go with the Pipes, and in the same way the man who receives the Pipes calls on his kindred to help in making the return gifts. These gifts all count in a man's tribal honors and are all made in the interest of peace and fellowship.

The Wa-wan ah-ka provides the two Pipes: these are ceremonially made, with secret ritual, are not used for smoking, have no bowl, and, are ornamented with paint and the feathers of birds, every tint and article in their construction being emblematic. There is a crotched stick, Zhan-zha-ta, for the Pipes to rest upon ; also two gourd-rattles, Pae-g' hae, and a bladder tobacco pouch, Ne-ne-bakh-tae, around each of which is painted a symbolic device, a circle representing the horizon, with four projecting lines indicating the four points of the compass or the four winds ; a whistle made from the wing bone of an eagle, Ne-thu-dae ; three downy eagle feathers, Hink-hpae, and the skin of a wild cat having the claws intact, In-g'thun-ga-ha. The skin forms the case or covering for the Pipes and the other ceremonial articles.

A Wa-wan party usually consisted of from eight to twelve men and they sometimes traveled over two hundred miles to reach their destination. They were never in fear of hostile attacks by the way, war parties turning to one side and letting the Pipes of Fellowship pass in peace.

The Wa-wan has been observed by many tribes of different linguistic stocks. Marquette, in 1672, says that the Calumet is "the most mysterious thing in the world. The scepters of our kings are not so much respected, for the Indians have such a reverence for it that one may call it the God of peace and war, and the arbiter of life and death." . . . "One with this Calumet may venture among his enemies and in the hottest battles they lay down their arms before this sacred pipe. The Illinois presented me with one of them which was very useful to us in our voyage."

Marquette's description of the ceremony he witnessed, making due allowance for his lack of intimate acquaintance with Indian religious customs, indicates that there has been little change in the Wa-wan as seen two hundred years ago among the Algonquin stocks, and its observance by the Omahas within the last decade.

The ceremony is replete with symbolism, from the rule which in token of humility restrains the members of the party from washing their faces, to the employment of the little child, Hunga (the Ancient or Leader), from whose hands the gifts are bestowed which count as honors to their donors, and over whose head the teachings of peace are delivered, and the groove along the pipe stem pointed out as the straight path bright with sunshine and happiness for him who will pursue it. Said an Omaha to me, "The eagle whose feathers deck the Pipes and the wild cat whose skin is their covering are fierce creatures that do not fail of their prey, but in the Pipes all their power is turned from destruction to the making of peace among men."

The movements of the Pipes represent the eagle rising from its nest and its flight on this mission of fellowship and peace; the songs constantly refer to the eagle, to the clear sky symbolic of peace and the good that is brought man by his becoming as one family, or as one of the song says "bound by a tie stronger than the one of the body"—meaning that between father and son.[1]

Song No. 32 was sung en route before the party dispatched the runners to carry their gift of tobacco to the man to whom they intended to present the Pipes. The words mean, "Whom do I seek."

As the messenger from the man who has accepted the tobacco approaches the Wa-wan party he is greeted with song No. 33; the words are, "This I seek." There is a double meaning in this song; it implies that those bringing the Pipes seek to give the assurance of peace to the gens they are to visit, and that fellowship is also sought by those about to entertain the Wa-wan party.

After due preparation the men move on to the village, generally about half a mile or so distant, preceded by the Pipe Bearers in ceremonial costume, and, as they near the village the Pipes are swayed to song No. 34, which is sung four times. All the Wa-wan songs are thus repeated. This song is the first in the ritual to mention the eagle. The words say: "We have reached there, the mother screams returning;" meaning, after our long journey we near the place to which we have come to bring peace and lay the Pipes at rest, and, as the mother eagle screams on her return, that her young may know of her coming, we sing as we come bringing peace.

Having entered the village the visitors halt, and after a few moments, again advance directing their steps toward the lodge set apart for the ceremony. They move to the beautiful song No. 35 that, once heard, can hardly be forgotten. The words are, "This is the one or only good," meaning, The peace and fellowship which I bring, is the one good gift for man.

At the back of the lodge a place is set apart for the Pipes where they are laid at rest in a ceremonial manner, certain forms, move-

[1] An account of this ceremony was published in the XVI Report of the Peabody Museum of American Archæology and Ethnology; years of additional study have shown a few errors in that narrative, which is in the main correct although not complete in all the details, or the bearing of the ceremony upon the tribal organization.

ments and positions being carefully observed. The Bearers take their station just behind the Pipes, and remain there during the three days and nights required for the full performance of the ceremony.[1]

The Bearer of the wild-cat skin lays it on a prepared space upon the floor of the lodge, and the Pipe Bearers sing the songs belonging to the ceremony of laying down the Pipes; the Pipes are swayed high over the skin, then sweep lower and lower, rising and falling and circling as does the eagle over its nest. With the final cadence of the last song the Pipes are laid one end resting on the skin and the mouth-piece leaning on the crotched stick, which is thrust in the ground at the head of the wild-cat. Under the feather ornaments of the Pipes the rattles are placed.

There are several songs belonging to the act of laying down the Pipes; two of the more popular ones are given, Nos. 36 and 37. There are no words except Hun-ga, and this refers to the important part in the ceremony borne by the child Hunga.

No. 38 is always sung at the final resting of the Pipes on the cat-skin and crotched stick.

When the Ah-wan e-ah-ka, the man who receives the Pipes, arrives in the lodge, the ceremonies are renewed; the Pipes are ceremonially raised, the Bearers lifting and holding them in the left hand, taking the rattles in the right—the Pipes are first waved near the ground, then higher and higher until during the final song they are well up and represent the eagle ready for flight.

Song No. 39 suggests the eagle stirring, and lifting itself from the nest; as the wind blows the branches of the trees, so the Pipes are raised and the song stirs the hearts of the people.[2]

Among the Pawnees it is the custom to explain many of the songs, that they may be more heartily enjoyed.

The highly poetic character of the Wa-wan songs and of this entire ceremony is native; nothing has been borrowed from our own race that I have been able to discover. The ethical teachings are in strict accordance with Indian ideals which here reach some of their highest expressions.

[1] The great change which has overtaken the Indian in his mode of living, his present farming life, prevents these lengthy ceremonies and one afternoon and evening is all that can now be given to the Wa-wan under the new conditions.

[2] The signification of these songs was given me by Indians initiated in the ritual of the ceremony. Although they are frequently without words, or with only fragmentary syllables, their meaning is inculcated and treasured by the people.

There are several songs belonging to the ritual of raising the Pipes. No. 40 is the one always sung at the close of this movement and its final exultant phrase indicates the eagle fully risen ready for the onward flight, which is typical of the sending out over the people the message of peace.

At the close of the song the Pipe Bearers turn to the left and with slow rhythmic steps, face the people sitting in groups close to the walls of the lodge, the drum follows accompanied by a few singers and the choral No. 41 is sung; the Pipes as they are borne past are waved over the heads of the men and women who join in the song, until the entire lodge is vibrating with this majestic hymn of welcome to peace. The words are few, broken, changed and elliptical : "This is what is given, what is brought to you —peace, brotherhood." "The Pipes are of God!" said an old Indian to me at the close of this song.

The Pipes are generally carried four times about the lodge, a new song is sung for each circuit, each song being repeated four times; a pause follows the close of the repetition of each song, while the singers halt for a moment. There is a large number of these chorals—some of them very spirited, some full and solemn, some delicate and tender as No. 42. The words are few. Kae-tha means the clear sky; een-tun-ee-nae, now coming. The meaning of this song was given me by Indians who were responsible and well versed in the ceremony. "The clear sky, the green fruit-ful earth is good, but peace among men is better." The music is faithful to the thought.

No. 42 A is a favorite choral.

Nos. 43 and 44 are prayers for clear weather. Traces of ancient Sun worship are recognizable in some of the symbolic adornments of the Pipes, and for the happy issue of the ceremony wherein peace and fellowship are sought, the blessing of sunshine is considered essential; therefore if storms come during the performance of the Wa-wan, the people cry for the happy omen of the sunlight. The words are broken and few, but the choral No. 44 is full and solemn.

After the lodge has been circled four times the Bearers stand at the back of the lodge facing the place assigned to the Pipes. Then follow the songs in the ritual of laying down the Pipes, and when the Pipes are at rest, speeches, gifts and other ceremonial acts take place. Generally the Pipes are taken up and the lodge circled

twice during the first three evenings ; the ceremonies of the fourth
night are different.

The examples of Otoe Wawan songs are of interest musically.
The first two, Nos. 46 and 47, are sung as chorals while the Pipes
are carried around the lodge.

The beautiful song No. 48 is sung as the Pipes are laid at rest.
It is a great favorite.

Nos. 49 and 50 are Pawnee songs. The Wa-wan music of this
tribe is good and often quite spirited.

On the fourth night the dance called I-man-tha is performed, but
if for any reason the ceremony of the Wa-wan is not to be complete,
it is brought to a close prior to this dance ; otherwise the final dance
called Ba-zhan takes place the next morning. The two dances are
similar in movement, but the latter must be in the presence of the
little child, Hunga. For these dances two athletic young men from
the Wa-wan party strip to the breech cloth, and take off the moccasins ; a red circle, typical of the sun, is painted on the breast and
back and a hinkh-pae, downy eagle feather, tied in the scalp lock.
The Pipes are handed to the dancers with certain ceremonies, and
they begin their dance, advancing and retreating, each one on his
own side of the fire, and waving the Pipe high over his head. The
movements are light, rapid, spirited and graceful; the songs are
different from any used in other parts of the ceremony and are
never sung except for the Ba-zhan or I-man-tha. During this dance
the Pipes may be challenged and taken from the dancer by some
one of the entertaining party, who recounts a brave act or generous
deed. He then lays the Pipe down at the spot where the dancer
was checked, and it can only be taken up or redeemed by some
one of the Wa-wan party who matches the recited deed from his
own experience, and restores the Pipe and the interrupted dance
is resumed ; much mirth often comes in play at this part of the
ceremony. In these songs there are generally two divisions, an
introduction and an accompaniment to the dancing movements.
As the dance requires great agility and strength it is of short dura-
tion. No. 51 is an example of these songs.

On the morning of the fifth day before sunrise and without break-
ing their fast, the Wa-wan party proceed to the lodge of the Ah-
wan e-ah-ka taking with them the third Hinkh-pae and the clothing

brought to dress the little child or Hunga. The Pipes, borne by the two dancers of the preceding night, lead the procession and the men all sing the ritual song No. 52. The words are : Zhin-ga, little or child ; the, you ; ou-we-nae, I seek. I seek you little child to be the Hunga.

At the door a halt is made and song No. 53 sung. The words are : "I have come, I seek you, child, it is you I seek as Hunga."

After this the party enters and one of the younger children of the Ah-wan e-ah-ka is handed over to the Leader to be dressed and painted. This is done by a man of valiant record. The face is painted red symbolic of the dawn, a black line is drawn across the forehead and down each cheek and the nose, indicative of the experiences of life and death. While the painting is being done, the Pipes are swayed to song, No. 54. The words are : Ah-tha-ha, adhere ; thae, this ; ah-thae, I make it.

After the painting is completed, while another song No. 55 is sung, eagle down is sprinkled over the child's head to symbolize the young eagle, and the Hinkh-pae, downy eagle feather, tied upon its hair. The words of this ritual song are : Ab-g'thae, I make it stand, Hunga.

The Wa-wan ah-ka or Leader of the Wa-wan party then selects a man to carry the Hunga to the lodge where the ceremonies have been held during the past four days. The man takes the child upon his back, keeping it in place by a blanket thrown around his own shoulders, and walks before the Pipes and the Wa-wan party who follow singing No. 56, "You have the Hunga." The Wa-wan ah-ka takes his place at the left of the man, who outside the door of the lodge sits with the Hunga between his knees.

All gifts made to the Wa-wan party are sent by children who advance leading the ponies, and are thanked by the Hunga who strokes the left arm of the messenger. Sometimes a man in full gala dress, well painted, his horse also decorated, will ride up in front of the Hunga, and there recount his valiant deeds, the drummers responding, then return to his lodge, and send back the horse as a gift by the hand of his little child. The day is often far spent before all the gifts of horses are gathered together. The ceremonial articles are left with the Ah-wan e-ah-ka who has become bound to the Wa-wan ah-ka and his gens, as a son to a father. The Wawan party hasten to start on their homeward journey, and camp half a mile from the village, where they cook and eat their first meal, after a fast of nearly twenty-four hours.

THE FUNERAL SONG.

There is but one funeral song among the Omahas, and it is only sung during the obsequies of a man or woman who has been greatly respected in the tribe.

Upon the death of such an one, the men in the prime of early manhood meet together near the lodge of the deceased, divest themselves of all clothing but the breech-cloth, make two incisions in the left arm, and under the loop of flesh thus made, thrust the stem of a willow twig, having on it sprays of leaves. With their blood dripping upon the green branches hanging from their arms, the men move silently to the lodge where the dead lies; there ranging themselves in a line, shoulder to shoulder, and marking the rhythm of the tune by beating together two willow sticks, they sing in unison the funeral song No. 57. There is a violent contrast between the bleeding singers and their vocal utterances, for the music in its major strains suggests sunshine, birds and verdure, and a fleet, happy movement; nevertheless there must be some latent harmony between the song and the ceremony. Music, as we have seen, has, according to Omaha belief, power to reach the unseen world. The spirit of the dead man can hear the song as it leaves the body, and the glad cadences are to cheer him as he goes from his kindred. He hears only, he cannot see, so the song is for him; the bleeding body is an expression of the love felt by the living, and the kindred of the dead can see the blood and note the manifested honor and sympathy. It is a custom among the Omahas to cease wailing at a certain point in the funeral ceremonies, for the reason, they say, that the departing one must not be distressed as he leaves his home behind him. And it is also customary after a death to lacerate the limbs, as the shedding of blood expresses how vital is the loss. The funeral song and ceremony, savage as they appear at first sight, are really full of tender unselfishness, and indicate a strong belief in the continuation of life and its affections.

III. INDIVIDUAL SONGS.

In this group, under seven sub-groups, are classed those songs that, in their origin, are expressions of personal feeling or appeal. They are sung either as solos, or by companies of persons who are about to engage in a common action, or who are united by having received, while fasting, visions of a like object.

Sub-group A comprises songs pertaining to war. These fall into four divisions:

(a) The Me-ka-se wa-a*n*, sung at the initiation of warlike expeditions.

(b) The Na-g'the wa-a*n*, used when the warriors are in the field and dangers threaten them.

(c) The Wae-to*n* wa-a*n*, chanted by the women in behalf of men on the war-path.

(d) The Wae-wa-che wa-a*n*, the song of triumph over the fallen enemy, sung after the return of a successful war party.

The songs of this group, although taking their rise in personal experiences or emotions, are not considered as the sole property of the composer, but can be learned and sung by the people.

Sub-group B contains songs of mystery which directly appeal to the unseen forces which surround man, and these arrange themselves in five divisions:

(a) The tribal prayer.

(b) Songs that came to a youth during his fasting vigil, at which time the Powers appealed to revealed themselves to the suppliant in some particular form; and songs thus given become the medium by which help and succor are asked and received in the hour of need. Later in life the man may ally himself to a society composed of persons who have received a similar revelation; for instance, those who have seen a horse in a vision are eligible to membership in the Horse Society, or those to whom Thunder symbols came can join the Thunder Society. Songs of this division while they are sacred to the man who receives them can sometimes be sung by members of the society to which the man belongs.

(c) In this division are grouped the songs that in dreams come to a man together with the knowledge and use of medicinal roots and herbs. Some of these songs have been handed down for generations, but neither songs nor knowledge is an inheritance, but is to be had by purchase only; even a mother will not impart to her children this use of roots without a *quid pro quo*. The songs belong to the acts of seeking, gathering and preparing the plants, they may be heard by any one, but nobody attempts to sing them as they are private property, and so respected by old and young.

Sometimes persons having knowledge of certain remedies assist one another in the management of cases, as the Buffalo doctors have been known to do. These men in a vision of Buffalo have received instructions concerning a certain remedy efficacious in healing wounds, to be applied in a particular manner and with certain ceremonies which include songs ; the Buffalo doctors are therefore specialists and treat only wounds. The songs and the medicine go together, and the former would not avail without the latter.

(*d*) These songs differ from those of the preceding division in that they are general in their benefits and can give the singer success in hunting, in war, or in any of his undertakings.

(*e*) The songs of this division bring help to the hunter or trapper ; they too can be bought, and must be sung after the traps are set or before the hunter seeks the game. They have power to entice the animals, and cause them to fall into the hands of the singer.

Sub-group C comprises Songs of Thanks. These are sung when gifts are publicly bestowed and received ; they are bought and sold.

Sub-group D comprises songs that occur in myths. They are the delight of the children who use them in their games and they form the only nursery music known in the tribe.

Sub-group E are the Wa-oo wa-an. These songs relate to the adventures and experiences of young men and women, and are somewhat of the ballad order.

Sub-group F are the Be-thae wa-an or love songs, sung by young men during courtship.

Sub-group G : Flageolet Music. The flageolet is the musical instrument of young men and is principally used in love affairs to attract the attention of the maiden and reveal the presence of the lover.

SUB-GROUP A, SONGS PERTAINING TO WAR.

(*a*) Me-ka-see wa-an : Me-ka-see, wolf ; wa-an, song. The wolf is the patron of the warrior ; the man on the war-path speaks of himself as a wolf. When a number of men have decided to go out as a war party, they meet together and perform the Me-ka-see dance and sing the Me-ka-see wa-an. These songs are also sung as the warriors leave the village, going forth on a long expedition, or when the party is travelling and in no immediate danger.

Song No. 58 was composed by the Leader of a war party when he had been a long time away from the tribe and all the men were homesick. The song, although giving vent to their unhappiness,

seems to have cheered the warriors, they persevered in their ad-
venture and returned to the village with trophies of their success.
The song opens with syllables expressive of war-like emotion over-
shadowed by memory of the home scenes. The words are : wa-oo,
women ; ah-ma, they ; wae-tha-he-ba, have gone for wood ; hoo-
zha-wa, are happy ; hte, really or very ; ma-thin-ah mae-in-tae,
they must be walking ; thae-thu, here ; wakh-pa-thin, very poor ; hte,
very ; mum-b'thin ah-thin-hae, I walk.

"The women have gone to gather wood and are having a joyous
time chatting amid the trees, while here very miserable am I walking" is the picture conveyed by the song which closes with war-like
syllables.

No. 59 commemorates a victory over the Pawnees, when an
Omaha war party divided, and, simulating peaceable white men by
swinging their arms as they walked, approached the Pawnee village,
and fell upon the people before they had discovered the ruse.

The words are : We-tun-gae, sister ; sae-sa-sa, trotting ; an-
thun-wun-ge-ha, follows me.

The women who accompanied the war party shared the dangers
and were awarded their portion of the spoils. The song refers to
them.

In the song No. 60, the warrior declares that he, like the wolf,
has no fear in venturing into distant and strange lands. The
words are few, barely expressing the sentiment, the music and syllables giving amplification. The song is liked by brave men, and
is quite spirited.

Me-ka-see, wolf ; ah-ma, they ; ma-zhan, land ; num-pa, fear ;
ba-zhe, not ; ba, like them ; hae-ge-mun, I am so. The words are
blended and modified in the song.

(b) Na-g'thae wa-an. Na-g'thae means captive : the warrior if taken captive goes to his death, therefore the word is to the
soldier the synonym of death. These songs are sung when dangers
threaten and death is near. They are sometimes sung by the
Leader to inspirit the men, or by individuals of the party, who thus
strengthen their own courage to meet death. No. 1, referred to
on page 13, belongs to this group.

No. 61 is a rallying song. Ae-de, there ; un-ga-thae-tae, let us
go ; ka-gae, friend ; the-tun-gae, your sisters ; nun-he-tha, frightened as in danger ; be-dan, when they ; thun-zae, but ; ma-thin-un-
ga thae-tae, walk let us.

Sisters refer to the women of the tribe who, if not defended, or if the warriors are unsuccessful, will be left exposed to the enemy; hence the appeal "*Hae!* Friend let us go to the rescue, your sisters are in danger, let us walk, *Hae!* Friend!"

The music suggests that the path of duty is not easy, the rhythm gives the call, the urgent appeal and the movement are fitted to the stress of feeling.

No. 62 expresses the willingness of the warrior to go forth to fight. He would rise with the dawn, and like the day increase in power, following his leader. Um-ba, day; edan, approaching; nan-koo-thae, hasten; hun-the-be-ga, take me; Nu-dan-hun-ga, Leader; ah-yae-zhum-mae-tho, they may have said.

The day is approaching, Hai! Nu-dan-hun-ga hasten to lead me forward.

Song No. 63 tells its own story—words and music being closely woven about the thought of death. E-bae-tan, to go around, as around an obstacle or to circumvent a threatened disaster; thin-gae, none; ish-ah-ga, old men; ma, the plural; wa-gun-za-be-dan, when they tell; shae-ah, yonder; he-be-tae, reached that first; ah-buz-zhe-tae, have not said; Nu-dan-hun-ga, Leader; tae-hae, the difficult, hard to accomplish.

There is no evading death. The old men have not told that any one has found a way to pass beyond it. The career of a Leader is difficult of accomplishment.

(*c*) The Wae-ton wa-an are sung by women in mature life standing before the lodge of a family, one or more of whose members are on the war path. The songs are accompanied by beats upon a raw hide, which serves as a drum.[1] These songs are spoken of as Wazhin-thae-thae; this word indicates that through, or by means of these songs, strength, power, passion is sent to the warrior assisting him to be victorious in battle. The family thus remembered bestow gifts upon the singers, who by these Wae-ton wa-an have helped the distant husband or brother in the hour of danger.

No. 64. The words of the song are few and used elliptically. Nu-dan-hunga, Leader; wa-shu-shae, brave; sua yae, are always; ae-de-he-ke, when he arrives. The meaning is: When one is a

---

[1] At the Sun dance among the Dakotas the song, sung at the beginning of that part of the ceremony when the men are tortured at the pole, is led by women who hold as they beat it, a raw hide, in place of a drum.

Leader he must always be brave, and when he (the one of whom
the women sing) reaches the enemy he will not fail to be brave.

No. 65.   This song is serious and replete with feeling; note the
change of time in connection with the meaning of the words.   These
are not easy to translate so as clearly to reflect the full meaning.
Ka-gae, Friend; tae-he, difficult; ha-ee thun-zha; they say but;
hae ish-ah-gae, the old men; wa-gan-za-be-dan, when they teach
or exhort; nu, man; tae, to be; tha-thun-ga ta-dun, that you are
to find out; shun-tha-the-shae, that is the reason you are going.
Friend! the old men in their exhortations have said, it is hard to
be a man, to be able to meet hardships and overcome difficulties;
to learn this for yourself you are now in quest of the enemy.

The words in No. 66 are few but full of assurance.   The opening phrases are accompanied by syllables only, so also the last
two, one phrase alone is supplied with words.

Ae-de-he-ke, when he gets there; wa-shu-sha, brave; meaning
when he, the warrior who has gone forth, reaches the enemy he will
be brave.

The words of Song No. 67 are difficult to translate literally.
Oo-hae-ke-tha-mae can be rendered by, "they gave him his way"
the obstinate person who persists in the face of the setting forth
by friends of the dangers that beset the course he wishes to pursue,
is at last left to follow his desire, to have his own way.   Wa-ba-
ska is a name that was used in this song while its possessor was
on the war path, but any name can be introduced; gha-gae, cry;
wa-tha-stan-zheah-dan-hae, did not cease.

He did not cease to cry, or plead, so they gave him his way.

The music of No. 68 is Dakotan.   The song was adopted by the
Poncas who supplied their own words, and the Omahas took it from
the Poncas.   It was sung by the Dakota women when the warriors
moved out of the camp.   As it is a foreign song among the Omahas,
it is sometimes used as a Wae-ton wa-an and sometimes as a Wae-
wa-che wa-an.

The words are Ou-ke-tae ah-ma, the tribes; the-nun-un-ta-
yae, that they may hear you; wash-konae gun-yah-hae, exert; yah-
hae is the woman's form of command.   Exert yourselves that the
tribes may hear of your bravery.

(d)   The Wae-wa-che wa-an are songs of triumph, sung when
the dance around the scalp of a fallen enemy is in progress.   Parts
of these songs are sometimes sung by women alone.

The music of No. 69 is quite expressive of the movements of one carefully making his way through the tall prairie grass, avoiding observation that he may successfully capture the horses of his enemy.

Sha-an zhinga, little Sioux ; shon-gae, horses ; the-ta, your ; ou-dan, good ; hoo-wa-nae, I seek.

Little Sioux, I seek your good horses.

No 70 is full of assurance and taunting and the music is lively and stimulating to pride. Oo-tha-zha-zhae-gan, you emulated ; in-tae-dae, and now, or in consequence ; tha-gha-gae, you weep ; ou-tha-dae, people ; the-shon, surrounding ; we-sna-hte, I only ; un-wun-shu-shae, I am brave.

You (the enemy) emulated me (the Omahas) and now you cry. Among the surrounding people I (the Omahas) only am brave—because you emulated my deeds, you weep for your slain.

Zan-zhe-mun-dae, the person mentioned in Song No. 71, was a very old man when the incident which gave birth to the song occurred. There had been an attack on the village, and the enemy had been driven off with such vigor that they were obliged to leave their slain on the field. As the warriors rode toward the dead to claim their honors, the old man, Zan-zhe-mun-dae, was seen coming as fast as his feebleness would allow ; they halted for him to join them, and permitted him out of respect to his age and previous valiant career, to touch the dead, and thus carry off one of the coveted honors.

The words ah-ma, he ; sha-ee, is coming, are the only ones used ; the rest are syllables.

Song No. 72 has reference to the Dakotas who were almost constantly at war with the Omahas during the present century. The words are modern, but the music is old ; the same is true of other Wae-wa-che wa-an.

Sha-an zhinga, little Sioux ; ae-ge-zhan-dan, because you have done so ; Ae-ge-ma, I have done ; ae-ah-tan, why ; tha-gha-gae, do you weep.

Little Sioux, why do you weep, because I have done what you have done, that is, the Sioux attacked the Omahas and killed some of the tribe, the Omahas retaliated and the Sioux lost some of their number. The song asks why they should mourn who have received the same treatment they gave to others.

SUB-GROUP B, MYSTERY SONGS.

(a) The Tribal Prayer, No. 73, is the prayer which is taught the child when he is sent forth to fast and pray alone, if haply he may obtain a vision which shall be a help during all his life. There is only this one prayer in the tribe, and it is applicable to all solemn experiences and important events in the life of every one. It is often heard when the lightning flashes, and the thunder rolls, and the singer goes alone to lift up his voice to the mighty powers of the air.

The words are Wa-kan-da, God; thae-thu, here; Wah-pa-thin, poor or needy; ah-tan-hae, I stand.

God! here, poor and needy, I stand.

(b) The spirited Mystery song No. 74 exemplifies the movement of the Horse, not any particular horse, but that creative power or force which is embodied in the form of the horse. This song may be sung in time of danger or when the man's horse is to be tested as to its speed or endurance. After the singing of this song the animal is supposed to be reinforced by the spirit Horse.

Nun-gae, gallop; sha-tha-mae, there they go; shon-gae, horse, weta, contractions of we-we-ta, my or mine; pa-hun-ga, first; thin, the; ae-ahma, they say.

> There they go galloping,
> My horse leading, they say.

The word ae-ah-ma, they say, at the close of the song, indicates that the man is not merely describing something he has seen, but something that has been interpreted to him to mean that his guardian, his especial spirit, would lead him and bring him to success.

In-g'than wa-an, or Thunder songs, belong to this subdivision. Men who sing these songs have in their visions seen the symbol of Thunder and heard the song which will have power to reach the god of the storm. By these melodies rain can be secured or the tempest stilled, and lightning may be called down to destroy man. These songs are also sung in the sweat lodge during purification, or when seeking to arrest death.

The words in Song No. 75 speak of the Thunder gods as "my friends" and their dwelling place or village is referred to and they are the gods who are speaking in the thunder.

E-ka-gae, my friends; e-ah-mae, they speak; Ta-wan-g'thun the village or people of the village; Wakanda, gods; ma, plural.

> My friends they are speaking
> The people of the village are speaking.
> The gods they are speaking.

Song 76 has no words. It is sung during the Thunder rites.

No. 77, contrary to the usual manner of rendering these songs, can be sung by nine old men, all of them Thunder dreamers, as they move solemnly around the camp circle generally during the night. The words are somewhat obscure, they speak of the Thunder gods going around, encompassing, circumventing; and declare that the gods make fearful, are themselves objects of fear to man. The music has a dramatic suggestiveness in sympathy with the vagueness of the words; the effect is heightened by the accompaniment of bells.

(c) Songs in this subdivision find their inspiration in visions which have conveyed to man a knowledge of medicinal plants useful in sickness or injuries.

No. 78 is sung by the Buffalo doctors when attending a wounded man—during the preparation and application of the remedy to the wound. The medicine is generally sprayed from the lips with considerable force so that it may reach every part of the lacerated flesh. The song indicates that this mode of treatment was inculcated in the vision.

"From here do I send it (the medicine to the wound) thus,—in this manner am I bidden to send it."

Thae-thu-tun, from here; thae-ah-thae, do I send; Ae-gun, thus; ne-thun, the water or medicine; shan-ah-dan, I am bidden.

(d) The songs belonging to this subdivision are potent to secure general benefits, and do not belong to any one avocation. ·The singer by means of this Mystery wa-an can achieve success in any of his undertakings. These songs can be purchased, but the selling does not preclude the use of the song by the seller. Several men may therefore use the same song.

No. 79 is an example. The words "walk this way" toward me, the singer, convey the invitation to that which he seeks, to yield to the magic of the song.

Du-da-ha, this way; man-thin, walk. These are the only words; the syllables carry the musical tones and fuller meaning.

(*e*) Trapping and hunting songs; sung after setting the trap, and before tracking the game. The songs are seldom elaborate in melody or rhythm.

SUB-GROUP C, SONGS OF THANKS.

There are quite a number of varied songs in this group, they are always sung in acknowledgment of a gift. When a poor man is remembered he generally goes outside the lodge and in the hearing of the entire village sings the song which tells of his good fortune, and proclaims the name of his benefactor. When gifts are made and received between men of equal standing, the songs are apt to be sung in the company only of those who happen to be present; at the same time, however, some old man less fortunate in his life who may have been the recipient of favors from either one of the parties, will go abroad to proclaim in a public manner the gifts that have been thus bestowed privately.

No. 80 gives an idea of this class of songs. The name of the giver is always introduced in the beginning of the second part of the song, followed by the words tha-un-tha-thae, you pity me, have compassion on me; win-tha-kae, you are true.

When the name of the giver is short, syllables are added to meet the requirements of the music.

SUB-GROUP D, MYTH SONGS.

These are bits of songs which occur in the myths that are told during the winter days and evenings; they are generally attributed to the animals who are so often the heroes of these tales. These melodies are sung by the women to amuse the children who catch them readily and in their childish way dramatize that portion of the myth wherein the song occurs, singing the melody with childish fervor.

When No. 81 is well rendered, there is much humor in the descending notes beginning with oh-hae-o, hae-o, etc., and the assertive conclusion "they have gone to the spirit," "they have gone to the spirit." The song never fails to delight all hearers.

Ma-stin-gae, rabbit; shae-tha-thin-shae, yonder going you; win-jae-ga-tha-thin shae, where are you going; wa-na-hae-tha-ba, they have gone to the spirits.

This group of songs has already been charactertized on p. 14.

No. 82 is the confession of a woman to the man she loves, that he had conquered her heart before he had achieved a valorous reputation. The song opens upon the scene. The warrior has returned victorious and successfully passed through the rites of the Tent of War, so he is entitled to wear his honors publicly; the woman tells him how when he started on the war path, she went up on the hill and standing there cried to Wa-kan-da to grant him success. He who had now won that success had even then vanquished her heart, "had caused her to die" to all else but the thought of him.

The modification and the choice of words and the use of the syllables indicate metrical feeling and expression.

> Nu-dan tha-g'the-*ah* dan
> Ae-tae-un tha-thae-thae
> Nu-dan tha-g'the-*ah*-dan
> Ae-tae-un tha-thae-thae
> Nu-dan tha-g'the-*ah*-dan
> Ae-tae-un tha-thae-tha *ya tha ya hi*
>   *Ha tha ha tha*
> Nu-dan snae-tae-de wa-kan-da wae-ka·tun-hae *thae*
> Wakanda ae-hae-ah tun-hae *thae*
> Ae-tae-un tha-thae-tha *ya tha ya hi.*

Nu-dan, war; tha-g'the-dan, when you returned; ae-tae-un, die; tha-thae-thae, you caused me; snae-tae-de, go when you did; Wa-kan·da, God; wae-ka-ah, I appealed; tun-hae, standing.

No. 83 is difficult to translate so as to convey its humor and sarcasm. The song purports to be sung by a man of the Don Juan type; he sits upon a hill overlooking the village, the murmurs of the people come up to him as they talk of his entanglements in uncomplimentary speeches interspersed with threats; he however shifts all responsibility, saying, "The gods have made me what I am" irresistible!

Ta-wun-gthun, village; thae-nun-yae dae, this many; un-thun-ge-ah, of me they talk; thun-kae, group; Wa-kan-da, Gods; hae-ge-mun-tae, what I am; in-thin-ga-yae, of me they decreed—h is added for euphony; ga-ma, yonder they; he-ah-mae, they talk.

No. 84 is derisive in spirit. An aunt, whose lover had left her and gone to her niece, acquaints the girl with the young man's previous attachment. He who so "skilled in speech" considers himself able to captivate both old and young.

Thae-thu-ta*n*, from here; sha-tha-yae, he went to you; we-tu-zho*n*-gae, my niece; e-ae, speech; tha-pe-ba, he is skilled; ha*n*-wa*n*-ke-ah, he spoke to me; Wa-ha*n*-thi*n*-gae, orphan, name given the youth.

No. 85 gives a glimpse into the life of a woman whose circumstances keep her from the man of her choice; she pleads with him to flee with her from the tribe and go to the Ponkas.

Dude-ha, nearer this way; un-dum-bae, me look at; nuz-zhi*n*, stand; ae-thum-bae, appear; ah-ya-nuz-zhi*n*-da*n*, I stand when; the-shna, you only; ou-we-b'the-zhe-dae, I look for you; ee*n*-u-da*n*, I am content; muz-zhe-hae, I am not; Ka*n*-zae-zhi*n*-ga, man's name; Ponkata, to the Ponkas; un-ga-thae tae-hae, let us go.

SUB-GROUP F, LOVE SONGS.

The Be-thae wa-a*n*, or love songs, are sung in the early morning about daybreak. The few words that are set to the music refer to the time of day. The young man seeks a vantage point and there sings his lay, the girl within the tent hears him and perchance by and by they may meet at the spring, the trysting place of lovers.

The syllables lend themselves to a flowing breathing sound, and the hand is sometimes waved before the mouth to enhance the effect by vibrations. The music is sung *ad libitum* as feeling may sway the singer.

No. 86 is very charming when sung with expression. The long notes suggest echoes, and the solitariness of the woods. The music is as simple and untutored as the flowers that are often the only listeners.

No. 87 is blithe and full of the joy of spring and the delightsomeness of youth. There are no suggestions of shadows in the song, no questionings, only a bubbling of happiness.

No. 88 is more serious in feeling, and there is a consciousness of nature, expressed in the music and of the passion felt for the object of the young man's affection. The few words are umba, day; e-da*n*, approaching, or dawn; hoo-we-nae, I seek you.

No. 89 is full of the movements of dawn, the gentle breeze that heralds the day, stirring the leaves, nodding the flowers, and awakening the birds. The youth comes forth with the light, his love overflowing in song, and the maid feels the day dawning in her breast; lovers, birds and the very sky are all in accord.

No. 90 would be recognized as a love song wherever heard; it is full of passionate fervor, and is worthy of recognition among musicians.

SUB-GROUP G, FLAGEOLET MUSIC.

Songs Nos. 91 and 92 are referred to by Prof. J. C. Fillmore. They, too, are the heralds of the lover who seeks his mistress.

INSTRUMENTS.

The instruments used to accompany the voice are the drum, the rattle and the whistle. The drum is of varied form and capacity, and is played in different ways according to the character of the song.

The small drum, about the size of, and similar in shape to the tamborine, is used in Mystery and Dream songs. It is beaten in tremolo by the fingers, or a small reed. Its rhythm is marked at the opening of a phrase, and the rapid light touch like the fluttering of the heart of a frightened bird, produces a stimulating effect upon the listener. This light drumming can be heard at a long distance in the night. Lying on the ground in my tent, my ear has caught the weird throbbing of one of these drums that some man more than a mile away was playing as he sang his song of the Supernatural. Listening to the sound and knowing its potency with the native mind, one can apprehend how this rhythm expresses the trepidation of man as he essays to approach the Unseen Powers that he believes controls his destiny.

The large drums were formerly made from the section of a tree, hollowed out, over the open end of which a skin was stretched. The drum was tuned by partly filling it with water kept sweet by charcoal, the skin being moistened, strained and dried to the desired tone. Drums of this kind are now almost unknown; a keg has been substituted for the hollowed section of a tree, and this sort of drum is used in many of the religious ceremonies. Large flat drums were constructed by stretching a calf skin over a hoop of wythes; these drums, supported by four sticks driven into the ground, were beaten with sticks muffled with leather. Our ordinary drum has now supplanted this particular native instrument.

The double beat. so peculiar a feature in many of the songs here presented, is played upon the large drums. In the drum accompaniment of the Hae thuska the accent is given with great force ; in the Wa-wan, the accent is not the less marked but the stroke is not as vehement as in the former.

The Indian drum answers to the rhythm of the human heart-beat as it responds to the emotion evoked by the song ; man's ambition and daring are aroused, and his social or religious sentiments are awakened. The variety of treatment and power of expression of this simple instrument as shown in Indian music are worthy of particular mention.

Rattles are made of gourds filled with fine or coarse gravel or pebbles, according to the tone required. A tremolo can be produced by shaking them, or they are played with a strong stroke and a rebound. The manner of playing them is determined by the character of the song. The rattles are used to accompany Mystery songs, and those of the Wa-wan ceremony, and are associated with the idea of an appeal to the Supernatural.

In presenting these Indian songs to her own race, the writer is conscious that they suffer in the divorcement from their own peculiar scene and circumstance. The music, to be understood and appreciated, needs its original setting of nature's colors, Indian life, and tribal ceremonial. This setting is always present to the consciousness of the native singer and his audience, it renders an introduction to the theme unnecessary, supplies the picture which stands in the place of an elaborated expression of the thought or feeling the song is intended to convey, and obviates the necessity of any prelude or elaboration either of the words or music. The words are always few, giving a hint rather than a clearly defined expression or narration, rendering it difficult for the unheralded melody to secure our attention or rouse our sympathy before it has finished its message and passed into silence. It is difficult for any one born and bred in our complicated social relations and customs to appreciate the openness and simplicity of Indian life, and to understand how all are under like conditions. There are no secrets, no hidden tragedies, no private sorrows in the tribe ; everything is known and seen by everybody. The directness, the briefness, the lack of preparatory words or chords, and the absence of subsequent unfolding of the ideas or feelings, which are so marked a characteristic of these songs, do not take the Indian by surprise or leave him unsatisfied. These songs—the product of Indian tribal life—suggest the question whether sustained thinking, without which there can be no full expression of thought in literature, music or any other art, is possible in a state of society where labor is not coördinated, where each person, each family, each gens must stand individually against dread hunger, and mortal enemies. The necessity of providing food and clothing is upon every man and woman, and the mode of living is such as to preclude the accumulation of property necessary to secure immunity from the pressure of daily needs, and the consequent leisure for mental labor and its artistic expression. While it is true that evidences of sustained thinking are wanting, these Indian songs show nascent art both in music and poetry. Moreover they reveal the fact that emotion in its simplest utterance weaves together words and melody and is unconsciously true to the laws which we have discovered to underlie and govern our separated arts of music and poetry.

In considering these groups of songs in their relation to Indian life, one is naturally led to compare them with similar groups among our own people. Taking a broad outlook over the two, one finds much in common in Indian and Aryan songs. Wherever one man yearns toward the mysterious unseen powers that environ him, whenever he seeks expression of his personal loves, hopes, fears and griefs, his song will answer in its fundamental directive emotion to that of every other man; this is particularly true of our folk music, which embraced in the past the Mystery songs, like the Ragas which controlled the elements, and other religious songs of our ancestors. When we bring the Indian song side by side with our more modern music, in which the intellect controls the expression of emotion, marked differences are shown, but there is a sympathetic chord and even some of the fundamental forms of expression, as the use of melody, harmony and rhythm, the grouping of measures, and the beating of one rhythm against another are common to both. The divergence is upon the intellectual rather than the emotional plane. Our music shows the influence of our social conditions, our coördinated society—our leisure class, whether this be sacerdotal or secular, and the added power gained through written music, wherein the eye has reënforced the ear, making the intellect more potent, and developing a new enjoyment and a broader field for musical expression.

The absence of certain kinds of songs among the Indians stimulates the inquiry, why, where so much is common between the races these should not be found, for example, the Labor or Guild songs, such as the old English Catch. These Catches originated in a society where labor had become secularized both in feeling and association. With the Indian, labor was not yet divorced from supernatural influences, the mystery of the fruitfulness of nature still surrounded the cultivation of the soil; he planted when the keeper of the Sacred Tent from the Hunga gens distributed a few kernels of corn with religious ceremony. The hunter and the trapper called the game by means of the Mystery song. In a word, prosperity by means of labor was not recognized as in the control of the laborer, but subject to favoring or disturbing occult Powers. The ground was still Mother Earth, the stones, the animals, the trees shared with man a common gift of life, and were his friends or foes. The Indian had not shaken himself free so that he could face Nature and bend her to his will; he had not yet comprehended the possibility of an intellectual, independent and external relation to the natural world.

In this contribution to the archæology of music it can be seen how far a people had advanced in the art of musical expression, who were living not in a primitive condition, but were organized in a social state where there was no class distinction or coördinated labor; where the food supply was still dependent in a considerable degree upon the hunter; where warfare was constant, and conducted by private enterprise rather than directed by a centered government; where the language of the people had never been reduced to writing, and where there was no possible training of the mind in literature or art. These songs therefore stand as a monument, marking the limit which the Omaha Indian's environment placed upon the development of his mental life and expression.

The Omahas as a tribe have ceased to exist. The young men and woman are being educated in English speech, and imbued with English thought; their directive emotion will hereafter take the lines of our artistic forms; therefore there can be no speculation upon any future development of Omaha Indian music.

REPORT ON THE STRUCTURAL PECULIARITIES
OF THE MUSIC.

BY JOHN COMFORT FILLMORE.

In the spring of 1888, Miss Alice C. Fletcher of the Peabody Museum of American Archæology and Ethnology of Harvard University sent me an Indian song which she had noted down from the singing of the Omahas, asking me some questions concerning its scale. A correspondence ensued which finally resulted in her commissioning me to make a careful scientific study of her collection of Indian Songs, several hundred in number. During the spring and summer of 1891, she also provided me opportunities of hearing many of the songs performed by Indians and of submitting to them my harmonizations of nearly the whole collection of songs.

My principal reliance in this work was on Mr. Francis La Flesche, an Omaha Indian in the service of the Indian Bureau at Washington, D. C. I spent a week with him in Washington, devoting my whole strength to the study of the songs. I afterwards accompanied him to the Omaha Reservation in Nebraska for another week of work. We were fortunate enough to find the tribe assembled in camp for the celebration of their tribal festival. We witnessed their dances, heard their songs, and their devotion and gratitude to Miss Fletcher procured for me the unprecedented favor of a special performance of the Wa-wan (Sacred Calumet) ceremony. This was given at her request, and on her account only, she being the only white person to whom such a concession had ever before been made.

A few weeks later Mr. La Flesche spent a week at my home, at which time we gathered up the loose threads and rounded up our work as far as possible.   To his unwearied patience, intelligence, courtesy and carefulness I owe much ; vastly more, indeed, than I can give any adequate idea of in any acknowledgment I can make. Without his devoted assistance, no thorough or complete investigation of the music of his tribe would have been possible.   No one else was so thoroughly competent in every way to assist a musician in finding out what needed to be known.

I also desire to acknowledge my obligations to Mr. George Miller, another Omaha whom I met on the Reservation, for his patience in repeatedly singing for me songs which Mr. La Flesche did not know, until I had noted them correctly ; to Mr. Noah La Flesche for a similar service in the music for the Indian flageolet, and to Pae-zhae-hoo-ta, Doo-ba-mon-ne and He-tha-ga-he-gae, the three Indians who conducted the Wa-wan ceremony.

In my investigations I have sought to cover the following points :

1.   The scales on which the Indian songs are built.

2.   The harmonies naturally implied in the melodies of the songs.

3.   The tonality of the songs as indicated by melody and harmony combined.

4.   Rhythms.

5.   Phrasing and motivization.

6.   Quality of tone and correctness of intonation.

7.   The Indian flageolet ; its scale, fingering and capabilities as a musical instrument.

1. *Scales*.   My first work on the collection of songs turned over to me was to go over them laboriously, picking out the tones of which each song was composed and arranging them in scale order. I found that a great majority of them were composed of the tones of the pentatonic (five toned) major scale, familiar in old Scotch, Irish, Chinese and other ancient music ; *i. e.*, of the tones of our major scale with the fourth and seventh omitted.   Some of them employed the corresponding five-toned minor scale.   But a very considerable number seemed capricious, in that they employed either the fourth or seventh and omitted one or more of the other regular scale intervals ; so that there were among them songs which could be reduced to major or minor scales of four, five, six, seven or eight tones.   The minor scale appeared both in its "pure" and "mixed" form ; *i. e.*, with a minor or major seventh, the latter being our so-called "harmonic" minor scale.   But there remained some very puzzling cases of songs whose tones could not be reduced

to either the major or the minor scale, whether complete or incomplete, because chromatic tones were employed. Such were the "Poogethun" song (No 8 of this collection), where the tones B and G # are introduced, the rest of the song being plainly in the scale of F; the "Taking away the Hunga" (No. 56) where A ♭ is used, the scale being G major, etc. If these tones could have been treated as mere chromatic bye-tones, they would not have caused much difficulty but the A ♭ in No. 56, at least, is an important melodic note; is principal and not accessory. So is the C ♭ in the song No. 32. These tones can easily be accounted for on harmonic grounds, but not by a reference to any known form of scale. But the Indians always sing in unison and never employ harmony. However, I hope I shall be able in the next paragraph to offer considerations which may point the way to the solution of the problem.

2. *Harmony.* Miss Fletcher had informed me of the curious fact that although the Indians never made any attempt at singing in parts, whenever their songs were played for them on a piano or organ, *they were not satisfied without the addition of chords to the melodies.*

This fact seemed to me significant and important. I thought it indicated the presence of a latent harmonic sense which might, unconsciously on their part, be a determining factor in their choice of melody tones. Accordingly I set myself to harmonizing a considerable number of songs, seeking only to employ the natural harmonies implied in the melodies. I then sent those harmonized songs to Miss Fletcher, requesting her to try them on as many Indians as she could, with a view to discovering whether they found my harmonies natural and satisfactory.

The result of the experiment was entirely successful. Whatever chords were natural and satisfactory to me were equally so to them, from which it seems proper to draw the conclusion that the sense of harmony is an innate endowment of human nature, that it is the same for the trained musician and for the untrained primitive man, the difference being purely one of development.

I have myself personally repeated this experiment many times and always with the same result. And since these melodic aberrations to which I have referred are easily and naturally accounted for by reference to their natural harmonic relations, *and in no other way,* I am forced to the conclusion that melody is a product of the natural harmonic sense and that all efforts to reduce primitive melodies to scales without reference to the natural harmonies implied in them must prove futile. I therefore spare myself the useless labor of enumerating all the specific varieties of scale to be found in these songs, regarding it as a wholly irrelevant matter.

The harmonizations given in the songs which accompany this report have all been submitted to Indian criticism, some of them many times, and have been found satisfactory. I have also experimented with different harmonies and have invariably retained those which the Indian ear preferred.

These accepted harmonizations give some curious results. The Indian ear accepts not only the major and minor concords, but the dominant seventh, as shown in most if not all of the songs ; the diminished seventh, as shown in the second measure of No. 63 (this chord was distinctly preferred to the dominant seventh in that place) ; sharp dissonances in the shape of suspensions, whether prepared, as in the twelfth measure of No. 41, or free (appoggiaturas) as in the first measure of No. 37 and in numerous other cases. These points cover pretty much the whole ground of modern harmonic structure. In addition to this, some of these melodies as, for example, No. 41, are clearly based on harmonic modulation and some of them, like No. 56 already cited, depend on third or sixth relationships. The chord of A ♭ in that song is the chord of the (major) under third of C, in which latter key the song closes, although it begins in G. This latter point, the use of the third and sixth relationships in harmony, is one of the most notable peculiarities of the Modern Romantic School.

.Practice of this sort is to be found in Beethoven and in Schubert ; more of it in Schumann and in Chopin ; most of all in Liszt and Wagner. That some of these primitive melodies, created by a people who never use harmony and who have no musical theory of any kind nor even a musical notation, should be explicable by referring them to a latent perception of these relationships and explicable in no other way, is certainly a surprising fact. It would seem to prove beyond question, if proof had been needed, that these relationships are primary and natural and that modern composers in extending the limits of the traditional harmonic system in which the fifth relationships had reigned supreme have simply discovered and utilized new natural materials and relations.

It seems clear enough that, as we might expect from what we now know, since Helmholtz' epoch-making work, of the complex nature of single tones, the primitive mind has, from the very first tone of a song, a sort of subconscious perception of harmonic relations and that these relations determine, at least in no small degree, the melodic succession of tones in the song.   Whether this subconscious perception includes the undertone series as well as the overtone series, according to the doctrines of Dr. Hugo Riemann and Prof. Arthur von Oettingen, I have not been able conclusively to determine.   The only fact which seems to bear on this question is that primitive man, in common with the trained musician, accepts the minor chord (so called) as a satisfactory concord.   And this chord, from the point of view of acoustics, is certainly not a concord in the overtone series and is a concord when referred to the undertone series and not otherwise.   But my experiments with the Indians have thrown no new light on the problem of the relation of Harmony to Acoustics.   It is clear enough that Indian musical composition is due to the impulse to express emotion in melodic and rhythmic forms and that the determining forces are imagination and feeling.   Of course this expression of feeling is conditioned on physical laws; but thus far I see no reason to expect, as I once hoped, that the study of primitive music may lead to further discoveries as to how far-reaching those laws may be. The fact may be noted, however, that major keys and major chords predominate in these songs, and that the Indian ear prefers a major chord, as a rule, at the close of a minor song.   All of which suggests that, even if there be a subconscious perception of the undertone series, the overtone series predominates over it, in their minds.

It is possible we shall sometime discover that the tones we hear are more complex than even Helmholtz knew ; that the undertone series as well as the overtone series is present in every tone, and that "major" and "minor" conceptions are due to the predominance of one or the other, much as quality of tone (*timbre, klangfarbe*) is due to the predominance of one or another set of overtones. But this is yet to be conclusively proved.

3. *Tonality.* Before I became convinced that a latent sense of harmony in the aboriginal mind played an important part in determining these melodies, I had found that the question of their tonality was often difficult, not to say impossible to decide from the melody tones alone.   A few illustrations will help to make this clear.   Song No. 72 (Wae-wa-chee) contains two sharps (F ♯

and C ♯). Ordinarily, therefore, we should say that its key
note is D. But note the build of the melody. It begins on C♯
(third space of treble staff) ends on the A below the treble staff
and omits the tone G. If it be in the key of D, not only is the
fourth of the scale omitted, but the song begins on the leading
tone (seventh) of the scale and goes DOWNWARD until it finally
ends on the Dominant (fifth). The trained musical ear, at least,
cannot but feel that this is a somewhat unnatural beginning. But
if it be assumed that the missing scale tone is not G but G♯, the
case presents no further difficulty. It is natural enough for a melody to begin on the third of the scale and go down. What is more,
if we think the song as beginning, in the key of A, there is no
difficulty in harmonizing it easily and naturally. Whereas the
first part of it can hardly be harmonized in the key of D otherwise
than awkwardly and unsatisfactorily, the latter part can be harmonized as well in D as in A, and the Indian ear prefers the ending in D. One would decide the tonality then, not alone from the
tones actually employed in the song, but from considering what
tone or tones needed to be supplied in order to make a natural and
satisfactory harmony. Thus, the question "What scale has this
song?" simply resolves itself into the question of harmony. If we
can decide on the Tonic chord, the scale will settle itself. And
the question of the Tonic chord depends mainly on the harmonic
implications of the melody. Scale, I have come to think, is an
entirely subordinate matter.

Take No. 67 for further example. It is in the key of A, beyond
doubt; yet the leading tone (G♯) is nowhere to be found in it, and
must be supplied in the harmony.

So I regard No. 17 as in the key of A, although it contains neither
the seventh nor the fourth of the scale of A. And No. 19 is in
the key of D, although both C♯ and G are missing. These last
two furnish admirable examples of pentatonic scales. It is curious, by the way, to see how many of these songs begin and end
on the fifth of the scale, as does No. 17. And many others end on
the fifth (among them No. 72, if we end it in D, as the Indian ear
prefers it), although they begin on some other interval, perhaps
the tonic, as does No. 19. This brings the tonic chord, at the close,
into its natural position when made up of three tones only, with
none of them doubled. Whether this peculiar ending is due to a
dim consciousness in the Indian mind of this natural position of

the tonic chord, it is impossible, of course, to say with the full assurance of certainty. But it is certain that the songs thus harmonized satisfy the Indian ear equally with that of the trained
musician. Can this be accounted for otherwise than on the ground
of a common perception? I think not. The difference, as it seems
to me, is one purely of degree, due to training in the one case, and
lack of it in the other.

The examples I have cited might be numerously multiplied if
necessary. But they serve to illustrate the point that the question
of tonality in these songs is a question to be settled by the help of
harmonic considerations and not otherwise. Any reader who is
interested will study the songs for himself. For others there is no
need to multiply illustrations.

But the case becomes stronger when we come to take into account the melodies which more or less plainly imply modulation.
Of these, the beautiful choral No. 41 is the most conspicuous example. The song begins in the key of 1 ♭. There is not a single
tone in the melody, except the E in the last measure but one,
which is not to be found in the scale of B♭. Yet the course of
the melody is such as to force on one the sense of a change of key.
It is quite impossible to harmonize it satisfactorily without modulating, especially considering the form of the ending. The harmony
I have given to it seems to me to be naturally implied in the melody and satisfactory. I tried numerous experiments on Mr. La
Flesche with the harmony of this song, beginning with the sixth
measure. His comments would run about thus: "This sounds
right to me up to that point; the next part is weak; now it is better,—but it isn't right yet; now it is right." The latter comment
was made when I played the harmony as here given. I also tried
it on Reservation Indians afterwards with the same result, so that
I feel justified in holding this harmony to be entirely natural.

In this song the original key is kept until the fifth measure, in
which the first clause ends with the relative minor chord. The
next phrase of three measures is in the key of E♭ (sub-dominant),
the third measure effecting a transition to the key of F by means
of the chord of G (over-third of E♭), followed naturally by the
chord of C (dominant in F). The last clause begins in F, modu-
lates to C, in the second measure and closes the period in that key.
This key, the major over-second of B♭, the original key-note,
would seem to be so remote as to make it impossible to preserve

unity within the limits of a short twelve-measure period. But the melodic flow is so smooth and the harmonic connections so natural that I, at least, do not get from it the impression of anything forced, harsh or unpleasant, nor, do I feel the need of a return to the original tonic. The whole choral impresses me with its beauty, nobility and dignity. Indeed, I know not where to look for a finer musical expression of noble, dignified religious feeling within the limits of the choral.

In No. 45 the principal key is A♭, but I found it impossible to harmonize it satisfactorily without introducing the key of the relative minor and of the dominant. It closes in the relative minor ; but the Indians prefer the major chord for the final, and it cannot be denied that the form of plagal cadence here given is very beautiful.

No. 56 seems to be an example of change of key within very narrow limits. The first two phrases, comprising only three measures, would seem to be clearly in the key of G, while the remaining two phrases, of two measures each, seem to be in the key of C, with a modification of the plagal close, the major chord of the under-third being used in place of the sub-dominant.

The Otoe song, No. 47, may well close our list of citations on this subject. In it, we find, at least according to current methods of reckoning modulation, the three keys of E minor, B minor, and D major, the predominant tonality being that of B minor. The ending with the dominant chord gives a peculiar feeling of incompleteness ; a feeling caused also by the endings of some of the other songs, notably No. 32, which ends with the supertonic chord. This last song is also notable for its employment of the minor chord of the sub-dominant, thus making it a "mixed major" key, as Dr. Moritz Hauptmann aptly named this kind of tonality.

These unusual endings remind one of Schumann ; I recall particularly No. 4 of the "Kreisleriana," which ends with the chord of D major (over-third), the key of the piece being B♭. Such endings doubtless serve the requirements of emotional expression and thus used, are, of course, legitimate. No musician, civilized or uncivilized, is under obligation to cut his feelings to fit the theoretical requirements of cadence. He has a right to express his feeling just as it is ;—if he can.

4. *Rhythms.* One of the most noticeable rhythmic peculiarities of these songs is the grouping of pulses into measures of different

lengths. Some of them group their pulses in twos or in threes throughout. But many of them have groups of an unequal number of beats. Such are the beautiful Mekasee song, No. 59 (twos and threes), No. 36, also twos and threes, No. 62, threes and fours, and others. No. 74 changes its measures from $\frac{5}{4}$ to $\frac{6}{8}$, the dotted quarter note in the second part and the quarter note in the first part each standing for a drum beat, at the rate of 104 to the minute.

This last song serves also to exemplify the syncopation of which these songs contain numerous examples. The song begins a half-pulse before the drum-beat, and the first measure of five beats is divided into five twos. There is also a syncopation toward the end of the $\frac{6}{8}$ portion. The first measure is syncopated, in that the drum beat comes on the first note of the second phrase, while it comes on the second note of the first phrase, the second phrase being melodically an exact repetition of the first. This song I found very difficult to note down from the singing, its rhythm being extremely complicated.

One of the most striking peculiarities of rhythm is the mixture of twos and threes in the same measure. The Mekasee song, No. 58, has two examples of this in the $\frac{6}{8}$ rhythm where there are two drum-beats in each measure, represented by dotted quarters, while the song has three quarter notes in the measure. This is the same rhythm to be found in the No. 20 of the Mendelssohn "Song without Words," in "Abschied," Op. 82, Schumann and elsewhere in the works of the modern romantic composers. But the Omahas carry this rhythm to the greatest length in the Haethuska songs. The Haethuska dances, as I have seen them, require the double-drum-beat, a strong pulse followed by a weak one. Against this many of the songs have three equal notes or their value. The drum-beat being represented by two eighth notes, with a strong accent on the first, the voice will sing against it now an eighth followed by a quarter, now a quarter followed by an eighth, now three eighths, now a syncopation, the quarter note crossing the drum-beat. Examples of all these rhythmic forms may be found in the Haethuska Song, No. 19, and most of the other Haethuska songs exemplify them more or less. That a primitive people, without any musical notation and without any *theory* of rhythm, should have developed such complicated rhythms seems to me very surprising. I know of no greater rhythmic difficulties anywhere in our modern music than these Omahas have completely at command in their every-day music. It seems to be as natural and easy for them to beat two and sing three, and that too in all sorts of syncopation and complex combinations as though they had received the most thorough rhythmical training to be had in any conservatory in the world. Indeed, I suspect that a great majority of conservatory students the world over might have a good deal of difficulty in learning to do what is to the Indians an every-day matter. And if white students of music had to pass an examination in taking down Indian rhythms from hearing them, I fear a good many would come to grief. Rhythm is by far the most elaborately developed element of the Indian music, and in this respect civilized music has not surpassed it, at least in the point of combining dissimilar rhythms.

5. *Phrasing and Motivization.* That larger phase of rhythm which is called *phrasing*, the grouping of measures into phrases and clauses and the correlating them into periods, is represented in these songs in quite as rich variety as is that grouping of pulses which we call measures. We are accustomed to think of the normal phrase as a group of two measures, less frequently of three, but these songs afford numerous examples not only of two- and three-measure phrases but also of four-measure, five measure and even larger phrases. In No. 19, already cited, the first three phrases have four measures each, the fourth has seven ; the fifth, sixth and seventh phrases have four measures each and the eighth six.

No. 17 consists of two periods. The first consists of two five-measure phrases and one nine-measure phrase, unless one chooses to divide the latter into a five and a four. (The odd measure at the end is a mere breathing space ; as also in No. 19.) The second period has a five- and an eight-measure phrase, or two fives and a three. The former division is perhaps more natural with the harmony I have given it, the final measures seeming to be an integral portion of the long phrase rather than a separate short one.

These two examples are sufficient to show the richness and variety of the grouping in phrases and the correlation of phrases in larger forms which characterize the Omaha songs. No one with the songs before him needs more, to call his attention to the point.

As regards "motivization," the building up of a melody out of modified repetitions of a short melodic phrase which serves as a model (technically a "motive"), Nature seems to have taught these people precisely what our professors of composition teach their pupils, and with marked success. Not only the two songs I have just cited as examples in phrasing, but almost every song in the collection, employs its first motive as a model and thus secures the prime quality UNITY. They all repeat the motive in modified forms and thus obtain VARIETY, without which Unity becomes mere monotonous uniformity. They all correlate their phrases into clauses; their clauses into periods and the larger ones their periods into two-period "Primary Forms" with a symmetry which is entirely satisfactory.

As for Contrast and Climax, the remaining two essentials of any great Art work, the dimensions of the songs are too small to admit of the former, except as it is included in the variety of the treatment of the motive and of the rhythm; and there seems to be, in most cases at least, a real culmination of interest and of effect, notwithstanding the curious fact that the melodies almost invariably descend in pitch, from the beginning to the end of each period.

That is to say, the fundamental requirements of a work of art are founded in the nature of things and of the human mind and are obeyed as unerringly by these untaught primitive men in their efforts to express emotion in terms of the beautiful as by the best of trained composers. The difference seems to be one of development merely. The Indians produce no long, elaborate musical forms because they have not acquired the power of sustained musical thinking. But their spontaneous expressions of feeling in tones are, within their limits, artistic.

6. *Quality of Tone and Correctness of Intonation in Indian Singing.* That many of the melodies in the collection accompanying this report are beautiful, I think no one will deny. But I think also that the general impression of those who have happened to hear Indians sing is that their songs, as given by themselves, are not beautiful; and I shall be obliged to admit that, in certain important respects, my own impressions confirm those of other observers.

Of sensuous beauty of tone I have heard comparatively little in Indian voices. Nor do I see how it could possibly be attained under the ordinary conditions of Indian singing. Take the Waewachee or the Haethuska dances for example. A half dozen or more men sit in the open air round a large drum, beating it with their utmost force and shouting out war or victory songs at the top of their voices. In the Waewachee songs the women add their

shrill voices at their very loudest and both men and women begin
at the highest pitch they can reach. There is a continual inter-
jection of war-whoops from the men, and of shrill cries in imitation
of the bird-hawk from women both among the dancers and outside
of the circle. In the Haethuska dances the men have strings of
sleigh-bells on their legs. All of these noises are symbolic and
deeply significant to the Indian, but of course serve only to con-
fuse, if not to repel, the musical sense of the casual white visitor.
There is more or less noise and confusion in the camp. The wind
perhaps blows hard; it generally does on these rolling prairies.
Often another company is singing, dancing and drumming at no
great distance. The songs are the expression of excited feeling
and the singers are stirred up almost to frenzy. Under such conditions the production of a beautiful quality of vocal tone is physi-
cally and morally impossible. The most beautiful natural voices
would soon be rendered shrill and harsh by such unrestrained
shouting and screeching out of doors in damp or windy weather.
Any one who desired to cultivate a beautiful quality of voice would
find it impossible for his ear to make nice discriminations in tone
quality amidst such a hubbub. Indeed, nobody seems to think of
paying any attention to such considerations and the very idea of
vocal *cultivation* is, so far as I am aware, foreign to the Indian
mind. The qualities which they esteem in a singer's voice are power
and penetrating quality. I have heard strong, manly voices among
them, and in the Wawan (Calumet) songs, these come out well,
lacking much of the shrillness and screechy quality I heard in the
war-songs and scalp-songs. But even here, the men sang *forte* and
fortissimo for hours together, out of doors, in the face of a strong
southeast wind, with an accompaniment of big drum and rattles.
What chorus is there in the world which could endure such a test,
and acquire or preserve a beautiful quality of tone, under such
conditions? Or how could beauty of tone even be thought of?

The same conditions which prevent the development of beauty
of vocal tone prevent also any nice discrimination as regards pitch.
There is in the Indian singing a good deal of inaccuracy of intonation; much less, however, it seems to me, than might reasonably
be expected. I have known many eminent singers (soloists) to
sharp or flat a good deal under unfavorable circumstances; some
otherwise good singers do one or the other habitually; and the best
choruses sometimes fall in pitch a full half-tone during the per-

formance of a single song no longer than some of these Indian
songs. I do not think these Omahas often varied more than half
as much as that from the true pitch in most instances when I heard
them, except when they rose to what was meant for an octave at
the beginning of the second part of a song. Then they often fell
short a semitone. This is saying a good deal when we take into
account that the drumming and other noise made so much confusion that it sometimes required very sharp listening on my part to
recognize a song with which I was already perfectly familiar. I
do not wonder that superficial observers find no melody and no
beauty in Indian singing. The melody is covered up and hidden
by overpowering noise. It is not always easy to extract the real
kernel from the rough husk which surrounds it, and those who go
to hear Indian music out of mere curiosity with no desire to penetrate to the core of it may very well find their surface impressions
unfavorable. They are looking for what is not there ; and what
is there of real merit is not to be found without seeking.

But there is another reason why casual hearers of Indian music
find nothing in it, and that is that they have not the faintest idea
of the meaning and spirit of it. To them it is mere barbaric noise ;
"all sound and fury, signifying nothing." But the truth is that,
to the Indian, many of these songs are the fervid expression of
his most sacred beliefs and experiences. The Wawan ceremony
is profoundly religious, its symbols are treated with as great reverence as any priest treats the crucifix or the Sacred Host ; all phases
of religious emotion are embodied in its songs. He who knows,
feels and appreciates this, who penetrates so far into the Indian
feeling as to be partly oblivious of non-essential accessories, can
begin to appreciate the feeling Miss Fletcher expressed to me when
she told me that she had never been so powerfully impressed or so
profoundly stirred by any music as by the Wawan songs, except
by some of the great Wagnerian music dramas. This Indian
music is the true and natural expression of genuine emotion ; much
of it profound, much of it high and ennobling ; and the better it is
known the more this will be seen.

If an appreciative and intelligent listener like Miss Fletcher can
speak with such enthusiasm of Indian music, notwithstanding the
deficiencies of Indian performance on the side of sensuous beauty,
much more ought it to make its natural impression when given
with a beautiful quality of tone, whether by singers or orchestral

instruments or by both together, as I hope it will be some day. The music, as such, doubtless will make its impression. Whether it can arouse such enthusiasm as Miss Fletcher's, when taken out of the religious ceremony to which it belongs, given by people who do not sympathize with the feeling which gave it birth and wholly separated from its natural accessories, remains to be seen. But these beautiful chorals will certainly always remain the expression of genuine religious feeling and I doubt not their merit will be recognized.

7. *The Indian Flageolet.* This instrument is made of red cedar, ornamented with lead run into grooves. The specimen now in my possession is twenty-four and one-half inches long. It is bored, as evenly as possible from the lower end to a length of about seventeen and one fourth inches. The upper end is bored down six and one-half inches. Each opening contains a narrow slit close to the partition between the long and short bores. The partition is made smooth on the top, a thin plate of metal is laid over it, having a long opening and a rider is tied down over the plate so that a thin sheet of air is blown through the narrow space between the partition and the plate into the longer bore, the surplus air escaping through a vertical aperture in the rider. The instrument is blown from the end. Its construction is therefore substantially the same as that of a small open organ pipe; for the stream of air blown in at the upper end and passing through the thin passage at the upper side of the partition impinges on the sharp edge or "lip" of the metal plate at the entrance of the long bore and thus sets the column of air in vibration. The diameter of the longer bore is about seven-eighths of an inch and that of the short one at the upper end is less than one-fourth of an inch. Inside it is doubtless larger. Close to the lower end of the flageolet are four small holes circularly arranged, the use of which I have not been able to determine, as they are never stopped. The holes in actual use are six in number. The lowest of these holes is five and five-eighths inches from the lower end of the flageolet and three and three-eighths inches from the circular row of holes near the lower end. The upper (sixth) hole is four and five-eighths inches from the "lip." The six holes are about equidistant each from its neighbors, the distance between each two being a scant inch.

No. 91, a flageolet piece which I transcribed in Nebraska, illustrates somewhat imperfectly the defects of this flageolet as regards

the key relationship of tones.   This piece seems to be in the key of
F♯ minor, omitting G♯.   But the fundamental tone of the flageolet
is nearer F than F♯.   The key relationship of the tones A, B, C♯,
D♯ and F♯ (fifth line) are tolerably correct; but the lower tone
being almost a major third lower than the A makes the piece sound
very badly out of tune.   The upper F, meant for the octave of the
fundamental, is about a quarter of a tone sharp.   The fundamental
is, of course, produced by closing all the six holes with the fingers.
The upper F the Indians produce by opening all the holes except
the lower one.   The true octave of the fundamental, or nearly so,
may be obtained by opening the fifth hole only and blowing with
considerable pressure.   But this I have not seen Indians do.   Blowing with less pressure produces the over-fifth of the fundamental.
The upper F♯ is produced by opening the sixth hole only and in-
creasing the wind-pressure.   A true minor third (A♭) to the fundamental, or nearly so, is produced by opening the first hole.   Opening the first and second holes produces B♭; opening the first three
holes produces C, but flat.   With the first four holes open we get
D; with the first five open, E; with all six open, F, but almost a
semi tone sharp.   All these values are approximate only.   The
tones used in this piece (No. 91) are all produced with the first
hole closed, except the upper F♯ which is produced as above described, and excepting, of course, also the fundamental.   In producing the A, the second hole only is open; the second and third
holes open give B, the second, third and fourth holes open give
C♯; the second, third, fourth and fifth holes open give D♯; all the
holes open except the first give F, or E♯.   It is the fundamental
which is most out of tune with the rest.   No. 92 illustrates the
same points.

I have made, as yet, no attempt to determine accurately the precise vibration ratios of the scale of this flageolet.   Such an investigation would be interesting, but has little bearing on the really
important relations of the Indian music, since the imperfections of
it are plainly due to the limitations, not of the Indian's musical
perception, so much as of his scientific knowledge.   The flageolet
is evidently built "by guess" and only remotely approximates the
Indian voice in accuracy of intonation.   The really instructive investigations in their music must be made, I think, in their songs,
which are not only the natural, free, spontaneous expression of
their musical conceptions, wholly unhampered by the defects of a

faultily constructed instrument, but greatly predominate in amount over their instrumental music. We must recollect that they have no theory of music whatever, and therefore their flageolet expresses nothing but a rude attempt at approximating tone-relations which the more flexible apparatus of the voice enables them to reach in their songs.

Summary. The results of the foregoing investigation may be summed up thus : The deficiencies and defects of Indian music are, first, lack of sensuous beauty of tone quality; second, uncertainty of intonation. There is apt to be more or less wavering of pitch under any circumstances and this defect is most pronounced in the Indian flageolet, which always gives out its tones in false key-relationship owing to its faulty construction. The more it is used, the more it accustoms the ear to false intonation and it is therefore fortunate that this instrument is never used to accompany Indian singing. The only exception to this is in the case of some of the love-songs; and it is precisely in these that the intonation in singing is most wavering and uncertain.

But it seems clear that, notwithstanding these defects, the sense of key-relationship and of harmonic relations as determining the key-relationship of melodic tones is at least subconsciously present in the Indian mind. For when the melodies are given in correct pitch and with natural harmonies the Indians soon come, to recognize and enjoy them.

The merits of the Indian music consist, first, in an elaborate, well-developed rhythm; second, in fresh, original, clear, characteristic expression of the whole range of emotional experience of primitive people. As such, this collection of songs must necessarily prove of interest even if they were less beautiful than they are. Those here given form only a fraction of those in Miss Fletcher's possession; and those she has are only a small percentage of the great number which might be collected under favorable conditions. But the older songs are rapidly passing away under the changing conditions of Indian life and must be gathered soon if they are not to be forever lost. It is greatly to be hoped that the work of collecting and verifying them may be pressed before it becomes too late.

The problems presented in the study of primitive music are two :

1.   The problem of the origin and function of music.

2.   The problem of the psychological, physical and acoustic

laws in accordance with which the musical phenomena have become what they are.

1. As regards the first of these problems, I, at least, can have no doubt that music takes its origin in the impulse to express states and movements of the sensibility. These Omaha songs mean *feeling* to the Indian, in all cases. Nine-tenths, at least, of the criticism I have received from Indians in my efforts to play these songs has had reference to emotional expression ; and there is not a song in the collection which does not express to the Indian as well as to myself and other white persons who have heard them, well defined moods or excited states of feeling. They had their origin in feeling and their function is to express feeling. And this conclusion I correlate with other similar facts into the generalized statement that the content of music is emotion. I am, of course, aware, that distinguished critics, chief among whom are Dr. Edward Hanslick and the late Edmund Gurney, maintain the opposite opinion. But this opinion I believe to be based solely on a misapprehension such as might, perhaps be easily explained by a proper definition and analysis of emotion, which I have not found in the works of any writer on the æsthetics of music. Even Dr. Hanslick, while admitting that music may express the "dynamic element" of feeling, fails to perceive that what he calls the "dynamic element," identifying it, as he does, with "psychical motion," is really emotion itself. And he overlooks also the fact that states and movements of the sensibility may be expressed so as to be recognizable without reference to the *ideas* involved in them.

It is true enough that music by itself does not and cannot express love, hate. anger, jealousy, revenge, etc., if we include in these terms, as we seem forced to do, the conception of two or more persons and their relations to one another. There is, of course, no musical equivalent for a man or woman or for the relations between the two nor for two men fighting, etc. But these ideas are purely of the intellect, not of the sensibility. The *purely emotional element* awakened by these ideas, and that alone, is expressible in music. And emotional excitement frequently, if not always, begets the impulse to musical expression. At least, the impulse to express states and movements of the sensibility in song is nearly or quite universal among all the varieties of the human race and it seems to me wholly unphilosophical to deny that the content of music is that which gives it its origin, which it expresses to those who produce it and which it also conveys to other minds.

2.   The second problem may be succinctly stated thus :   What determines the particular form of musical expression?

From the psychological point of view it may be answered that the content determines the form ;   *i. e.*, the feeling which the primitive man is impelled to express in song finds its own mode and means of expression spontaneously.   This Omaha music illustrates this admirably ; for Indian song is an absolutely spontaneous natural product.

But there remains the further question : What correlations of the mind with the auditory and vocal apparatus and of these with the physical laws of acoustics determine the course of melody?   Under this head numerous questions immediately suggest themselves in view of the observed facts.   For example, how does it happen that, not only among the Omaha and other Indians, but also among the Chinese, the primitive Scotch, Irish, Negroes, etc., the impulse to express emotion in song should so frequently result in melodies based on the five-toned scale?   What facts and laws determine the development of this into the full scale of eight tones in common use?   What determines aberrations from this scale, such as are found in various songs of this collection?   What determines the choice or the preponderance of major or minor?   Is there anything in the facts of primitive music which will help us to determine whether the minor chord is a perfect or imperfect concord?   If the former, does it depend on some acoustic principle opposed to that which generates the major chord, or not?   These are all questions of importance in the fundamental science of music, none of which can be regarded as settled in any way which commands universal acceptance.

I have already pointed out that my experience during this investigation has led me to think that the fundamental fact which is to point the way to the solution of some, at least, of these questions is that the harmonic sense is universal.   It seems clear to me that the course of these melodies can be accounted for in no other way than on the assumption that the Indian possesses the same sense of a tonic chord and its attendant related harmonies that we do ; although, of course, it is latent and never comes clearly forward into his consciousness.   The five-toned (major) scale, exemplified

so numerously in this collection of songs, may be regarded, as a
tonic chord with two bye-tones, one of which belongs to the dominant and the other to the sub-dominant chord. At first, perhaps,
there is merely a feeling for the tonic chord, arising from the complex nature of a single tone with its consonant overtones.   The
two bye-tones, are perhaps, in this stage, merely used to partially
fill up the gaps between the tones of the tonic chord, which is often
implied in the initial melody tone.   The dim perception of the
harmonic relations of these two tones would seem to be a later development which results in the addition of the missing fourth and
seventh tones of the scale.   How the feeling for the tonic chord is
generated in melodies which do not begin with the key-note, and
especially in those which begin with a bye-tone, as some of these
songs do, I am, as yet, unable to conjecture.   Nor am I, at present,
able to discuss the other questions here raised more fully than I
have already done.   But I hope further investigation may fully
disclose the natural laws which govern these phenomena and I am
strongly in hopes that the suggestions here offered may prove fruit-
ful.

OMAHA SONGS.

No. 1.

NA-G'THAE WA-AN.

RALLYING SONG IN FACE OF DEATH.

No. 2.   WA-OO WA-AN.

No. 3. HUBAE WA-AN.

SACRED POLE SONG.

No. 4. HUBAE WA-AN.

SACRED POLE SONG.

No. 5. **HUBAE WA-AN.**

HAE-DE-WA-CHE CALL.

Zha - wa e - ba e - ba ha æ - hæ . . .

Drum.

Trundo.

Ped.

Zha - wa e - ba e - ba ha æ - hæ . . . .

No. 6. **HUBAE WA-AN.**

HAE-DE-WA-CHE DANCE.

Hæ hæ-hæ wa - na - shæ ah æ-hæ wa - na - shæ ah

Ped.

hæ hæ-hæ wa - na - shæ ah æ-hæ wa - na - shæ ah.

No. 7.

HUBAE WA-AN.
TENT OF WAR SONG.

The-te - gan num - pae - wa - thæ ga The-te - gan num-

pæ - wa - thæ ga. The - te - gan num - pæ - wa -

- thae ga. The - te - gan wae - tin kae g'the - hun ke num - pae-

wa - thae ga. The-te - gan num - pae-wa - thae ga.

No. 8. POO-G'THU*N* WA-A*N*.

No. 9.　　　POO-G'THU*N* WA-A*N*.

Shu - pe - da hu - ah - ta na-zhi*n*,*thae* Shu - pe - da hu-

Con Ped.

- ah - ta na-zhi*n*, *thae ah ae thae tha ae thae he thae.*

Ae - hae Hu- ah - ta na-zhi*n thae ae thae tha ae thae he thae.*

No. 10.　　　POO-G'THU*N* WA-A*N*.

Shu - pe - da*n* wea - wa - ta tha - wa- thae, Shu - pe - da*n* wea - wa - ta

Con Ped.

tha-wa-thae, Pa - tha - ga - ta tha - wa-thae. *ah hae thae he thae ah he thae.*

No. 11.   HAE-THU-SKA WA-AN.

Mysteriously.
Double beat. ♩ = 138.

Nun-g'thae thae - tae   he-tha-ke-un - tae   thunah-he - dae.

Con Ped.

Nun-g'thae thae-tae   he-tha-ke-un - tae thunah-he-dae. Nun-g'thae thae-tae,

he-tha-ke-un-tae thunah-he-dae. Nun-g'thae thae - tae   he-tha-ke-un - tae

thunah-he - dae. Nun-g'tha thae-tae   he-tha-ke-un-tae thunah-he-dae.

No. 12.   **HAE-THU-SKA WA-A*N*.**

PRAYER OF WARRIORS.

Religioso.
Double drumbeat. ♪ = 138. *Song.* ♩. = 69.

Wa-ka*n*-da tha-ne-ga thae kae, Wa-ka*n*-da tha-ne-ga thae kae, Wa-ka*n*-da tha-ne-

ga thae kae, *aeha* Tha - ne hin-ga *wae tho hae*   tho. ie   tho.

No. 13.   **HAE-THU-SKA WA-A*N*.**

CALL TO CEREMONIAL REPAST.

Smoothly.
♩ = 66.

Ou-ha*n* thae-tae ne-daeah tho, Ou-ha*n* thae-tae ne-daeah tho, En-da-coo-tha ne-dae tho,

Repeat ad lib.

Ou-ha*n* thae-tae ne-daeah tho, *hae*   *ae*   En-da-coo-tha ne-dae tho   *hae*   tho.

No. 14.   # HAE-THU-SKA WA-AN.

SONG OF DISMISSAL. CHORAL SONG OF WARRIORS.

With dignity and feeling.

Double Drum beat. ♩ = 116.

ff

Hin - da - koo-tha   na - zhin thae, Hin-da - koo-tha   na - zhin thae   Hin -

Con. Ped.

da - koo-tha na - zhin thac,   ae - ha   na - zhin   he - tha-mae *tho*

hae   *tho-e*   Hin -da - koo-tha   ma - thin thae.   Hin -

da - koo-tha   ma - thin thae.   Hin - da - koo-tha   ma - thin thae   ae -

ha   Ma - thin   he - tha *mae   tho   hae*   *tho.*

No. 15.   **HAE-THU-SKA WA-AN.**

Moderato. Martial.

Double beat.

Zhin-thae sha - e-ba-dan, Zhin-thae sha - e - ba-dan, Nun - dae wae - ga -

Con Ped.

thun - ga ta - ba - dan,   Zhin-thae sha - e - ba-dan. *tho hae*

tho - e.   Ta - hae-zhin-ga Hae - thu-ska ga - hae-dan   Nun-dae wae -

ga-thun - ga ta - ba - dan   Zhin-thae sha-e - ba-dan. *tho hae*   *tho.*

No. 16. HAE-THU-SKA WA-A*N*.

With feeling. ♩ = 56.

Hae-thu-ska thin-ga-bae, Hae-thu-ska thin-ga-bae, Hae-thu-ska thin-ga-

Con Ped.

bae, Gha-gae-ah thin-bae. *tho   hae   thoe.*   Te-thu the-sha*n* thin-ga-

bae, Hae-thu-ska   thin-ga-bae Gha-gae-ah thin-hae. *tho   hae   tho.*

No. 17. HAE-THU-SKA WA-A*N*.

Martial feeling.

Double Beat. Drum. ♪ = 160.   *Song.* ♩. = 80.

Tu*n*-gae-ah da - du*n* na*n* - tha-pae   he - we - tha - ga,   Tu*n*-gae-ah

Drum.

Ped.

No. 18.   HAE-THUSKA WA-AN.

RESTING SONG.

Song. ♩. = 72.

Um - ba thae - na   un - ge - tun - ba - ga   Um - ba   thae -

Con Ped.

na   un - ge - tun   ba - ga   Tun-gae   Um - ba   thae - na   un - ge - tun

ba - ga   *tho   hae . .   thoe*   Hae - thu - ska

na   tae - he - ae - dae   Pa - hae - tae   ah - ke - he - b'tha   Um -

ba   tha - na   un - ge - tun - ba - ga   *tho   hae   tho.*

No. 19.   HAE-THU-SKA WA-AN.

94

No. 20.　　　HAE-THU-SKA WA-AN.

Martial, with feeling.

Song. ♩. = 60.　Drum beat. ♪ = 120.

Ho -e ya ae ho oh wae ho e ya ae ho oh wae Ho

pp
Drum.

Con Ped.

e ya ae ho oh wae Ho e ya ae ho oh wae Ho

e ya tho ha oh wae tho hae . . tho-e.　Zhin-

ga - wa-shu-shae We - gee - the - thae dan wa - nun- hae

man-b'thin-ah tho shu - b'the-ah thin-ha. Wae tho hae tho.

No. 21. HAE-THU-SKA WA-A*N*.

With solemnity.

Han - thi*n*-gae ae-ah-ma, Ha*n*-thin-gae ae-ah-ma, Han-

Drum.pp

thi*n*-gae ae-ah-ma, Wa-kan-da thin-gae ae-ah-ma, Han-

thin - ga. *wae - tho hae . . . tho-e* Han-thin - gae

ae-ah-ma, Ha*n*-thin-gae ae-ah-ma, Wa-kan-da thin-gae

ae-ah-ma, Ha-thin-ga. *Wae tho hae . . . tho.*

No. 22. HAE-THU-SKA WA-A*N*.

Dirisive, with spirit.

Ah- tan tan-bae - da*n* shae-ga*n* ah-thi*n* -hae no, Ah - ta*n* tan-bae - da*n* shae - ga*n* ah-thi*n*- hae no. Ah- ta*n* tan - bae- da*n* shae - ga*n* ah-thi*n*- hae no. *hae* *tho-e.* Gha - gae - wa- thae wa - oo hae - the - ga*n*-ae Ah - ta*n* tan-bae-da*n* shae-ga*n* ah-thin-hae no, Ah - ta*n* tan-bae da*n* shae-ga*n* ah-thi*n*-hae no *hae* *tho.*

Con Ped.

No. 23.　　HAE-THU-SKA WA-A*N*.

No. 24. HAE-THU-SKA WA-A*N*.

DANCE SONG.

Light and spirited.

Ne-ka we-ta wa-gun-tha te-bae-no, Ne-ka we-ta wa-gun-tha

te-bae-no, Ne-ka we-ta wa-gun-tha te-bae-no, Ne-ka we-ta

wa-gan-tha te-bae-no, Ne-ka we-ta wa-gun-tha te-bae-no,

tho - e Nu-dan-hu-gan Ish-e-buz-zhe tha-da - e thin-

NOTE. — The Indians usually sing the second part of this song in the Key of G. But when I played it in A flat for Mr. La Flesche, he declared it correct, although I had heard him sing it in G. This shows that the interval aimed at, in going from the first to the second part, was an octave. But D was easier to reach than the upper E flat, and the Indian ear does not make nice discriminations. — J. C. F.

kae - dae, Ne-ka we-ta wa-gun-tha te-bae-no, Ne-ka we-ta

wa-gun-tha te-bae-no, Ne-ka we-ta wa-gun-tha te-bae-no.

No. 25.   TOKALO WA-A*N*.

Majestic.

♩ = 60.

ff

ff

Hae   ha   hae   ha ah Hae   ka   hae   ha ah   ha ah

Con Ped.

Hae   he tha*'* ka ah ha ah he tha ah   e tha   e   tha hae.

No. 26.

IN-OU-TIN.

GAME SONG.

Ha - ah ah ho - e tha ah Ha - ah ah ho - e tha ah

Con Ped.

Ha - ah ah ho - e tha ah Ha - ah ah ho - e tha E - ae-zhin-ga

da - dan skha-hae. Ha - ah ah ho - e tha ah Ha - ah ah ho - e tha.

No. 27.

IN-OU-TIN.

GAME SONG.

Con. Ped

No. 28. IN-OU-TIN.
GAME SONG.

E ya ha-e ha-e tha-e ya ha-e ho-e tha-e ya ha-e ho-e tha-e

Con Ped.

ya ha-e ho-e tha. E ya ha-e ho-e tha-e ya ha-e ho-e tha-e

ya ha-e ho-e tha-e ya ha-e ho-e tha-e ya ha-e ho-e ya.

No. 29.

IN-OU-TIN.
GAME SONG. SUCCESS.

Ka-gae ha - ta-ah- dan ansua zhin-ga, *hae thae* Ka - gae ha - ta-ah-

dan ansna zhin-ga, *hae thae* Ka-gae ha - ta - ah-dan ansna zhin-ga, *hae thae.*

No. 30. CHILDREN'S SONG FOR "FOLLOW MY LEADER."

No. 31.

HAE-KA-NE DANCE.
OTOE.

Song. ♩. = 100. *Double Drum-beat.* ♪ = 200.

Ha yo wa nae ho yo wa nae hae Hae
Drum.

Con Ped.

hae   ho   ya nae Ha yo wa   nae   hae   hae

Repeat ad lib.

hae   ho   ya nae Ha yo wa   nae   hae.

No. 32.   WA-WA*N* WA-A*N*.
EN ROUTE.

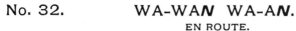

Ha-wa-thin ho-wa-nae   Ha-wa-thin ho-wa-nae   Ha-wa-thin ho -wa-nae   Ha-

- wa-thin ho -wa-nae   Ha-wa-thin ho-wa-nae Hae- wa-thin ho-wa - nae.

No. 33.

WA-WAN WA-AN.

RECEIVING THE MESSENGER.

No. 34.

WA-WAN WA-AN.

NEARING THE VILLAGE.

No. 35. **WA-WAN WA-AN.**

SONG OF APPROACH.

Thae-nan ho - dan thae-nan ho - dan thae-nan ho - thae-nan

ho - dan *tha hae* thae-nan ho - thae-nan ho - dan thae-nan ho -

dan Hun - ga thae-nan ho - dan *tha hae*

thae-nan ho - thae-nan ho - dan thae-nan ho - dan Hun - ga.

No. 36.   WA-WAN WA-AN.

LAYING DOWN PIPES.

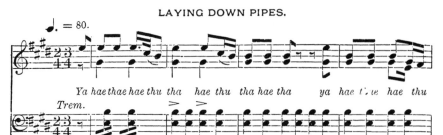

Ya hae thae hae thu tha   hae thu tha hae tha   ya hae t'ie hae thu

tha hae thu tha   hae thu tha hae tha   ah hae thae hae thu   tha   hae thu

tha hae tha   hae thu tha heah o tha   he thu tha   he   thu tha he   tha

No. 37.   WA-WAN WA-AN.

LAYING DOWN PIPES.

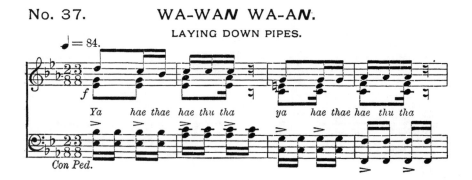

Ya   hae thae hae thu tha   ya   hae thae hae thu tha

ya   hae thae hae thu tha   ah   hae thae hae thae hae thu tha

ya   hae thae hae thu tha   ya   hae thae hae thu tha.

Trem.

No. 38. WA-WAN, WA-AN.

LAYING DOWN PIPES.

♩ = 88.

Heah   o tha ae o   hae   ha   Heah   o tha   ae   o   hae   ha

Trem.

Ped.

Heah   o tha ae o   hae   ha   Heah o   tha ae o   hae Hun - ga.

No. 39.

WA-WAN, WA-AN.
RAISING OF THE PIPES.

No. 40.

WA-WAN, WA-AN.
FINAL SONG WHEN RAISING THE PIPES.

ae ha tha wae tha wae ha . . tha Thae ah wae ho wae.

No. 41. CHORAL. WA-WAN WA-AN.

With religious feeling. AFTER PIPES ARE RAISED.

Thae ah-wa-kae-dea heah-oo-tha heah-oo-tha tha-kae - dae heah-

Double Drum-beat.

oo-tha Thae ah-wa - kae-dae heah *thae hae* Heah-oo-tha

ah - kae-dae heah - oo tha ah-wa - kae-dae heah-*thae hae.*

* N. B.   This and the other syncopations in this choral are struck by the Indians about a quarter of a tone above pitch. Both Miss Fletcher and myself noted them down as grace-notes; but they never satisfied Mr. La Flesche.   But when I played them as plain syncopations he at once expressed the most emphatic approval, saying that now, at last, they were correct. **J. C. F.**

No. 42. **WA-WAN WA-AN.**

Flowingly, with feeling. **AROUND THE LODGE.**

Double Beat. ♪ = 126.

Kae - tha   yah   Hun - ga   Kae-tha   Hun-ga een-tun-ee-nae

Con. Ped.

yah   Hun - ga   Kae-tha   Hun-ga een-tun - ee - nae   *thae*

Hun - ga   *Heah tha*   Kae -tha   Hun-ga een-tun-ee-nae

ya ah Hun - ga   Kae-tha   Hun-ga een-tun-ee-nae   *thae* Hun - ga.

No. 42a.   WA-WAN, WA-AN.

No. 43.   WA-WAN, WA-AN.
PRAYER FOR CLEAR WEATHER.

Hun-ga   Kae - e - tha *wae tha*   Hun-ga   Kae-e-tha *wae tha*   Hun-ga.

No. 44.   WA-WA*N*, WA-A*N*.

With dignity.

PRAYER FOR CLEAR WEATHER.

Double Beat. ♪ = 126.

Kae-tha Kae - tha Kae - tha *ha*   *heah-o*   *tha*   Kae-tha Kae-

tha   *ha*   *ya nae ho*   Kae-tha *ah* Kae-tha *o ha*   *heah o* *tha*

Kae-tha *ah* Hun-ga *ah ha*   *Heah o*   *tha ah*   Kae-tha Kae-tha *o ha*

ya-nae ho   Kae-tha *ah* Kae-tha *o ha*   *heah o tha*   Kae-tha *ah* Hun-ga.

No. 45.

WA-WAN, WA-AN.

RAISING THE PIPES.

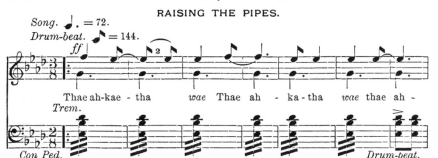

Song. $\quad \downarrow . = 72.$
Drum-beat. $\quad \downarrow = 144.$

Thae ah-kae - tha   wae Thae ah - ka - tha   wae thae ah -

kae - tha   wae Thae ah-kae - tha   wae tha kae - tha   wae thae

ah - wa - kae - tha   wae   kae - tha   wae   Thae ah - kae - tha

wae tha kae tha wae Thae ah - wa kae-tha   tha.

WA-WAN WA-AN.

OTOE.

No. 47. WA-WAN, WA-AN.

OTOE.

No. 48. WA-WAN, WA-AN.

OTOE.

No. 49.

WA-WA*N*, WA-A*N*.

PAWNEE.

No. 50.

WA-WA*N*, WA-A*N*.

PAWNEE.

No. 51.   **WA-WA*N* WA-A*N*.**

INTRODUCTION TO FINAL DANCE.

Ka - wae tha ka - wae tha ka - wae tha ka - wae tha kae ah wae tha kae ah

kae tha ka-wae tha ka wae tha ka wae tha ka kae ah wae tha kae ah kae tha ka wae tha.

♪ = 160.

ritard.

Ka-wae tha ka - wae tha wae   ka wae tha ka wae tha ka wae tha

a tempo.

wae   ka wae tha ka wae tha wae   ka wae tha   ka wae tha ka wae tha wae ka wae

♩ = 192.

tha wae ka wae tha ka wae tha wae   ee-the ka wae tha tha kae tha wae.

Drum-beat.

118

Very slight pause.

TwoVoicesonly.

ho kae tha ho kae tha o ha kae tha hae Ho kae tha ho kae tha

o ha kae tha hae ho kae tha ho kae tha o ha kae tha hae.

No. 52. WA-A**N** WA-A**N**.
GOING FOR THE HU*N*GA.

♪ = 168.

Zhin-ga the ou-we-nae Hun-ga Zhin-ga the ou-we-

nae Hun-ga the ou-we-nae Hun-ga Zhin-ga the ou-we-nae Hun-ga.

D. C. ad lib.

No. 53.   **WA-WA*N*, WA-A*N*.**

AT THE DOOR.

D. C. ad lib.

no   tho   Hun-ga ha-ne   no   tho   Hun-ga ha -ne.

No. 57.   **FUNERAL SONG.**

Smoothly, with feeling.

♪ = 96.

E ah tha ha ah   e   tha   hae ah hah ha   ah   hae ah ah   ah   e tha ah

Con Ped.

ah   ee   hae ah ha ah   ah   e   tha ha ah   e   tha   ah   e ah   ha

ae ha o   e tha   hae   hae   thoe   ha   o   o   e tha ha tha   hae ah ha ah   ah

e tha ha ah   e   tha   ah   e   ah ha   ae ha o   e   tha hae   tho.

No. 58.　　　　ME-KASEE.

Yaw ah　ha　yaw　ah　ha　ah yaw ah　ha　ah　yaw ah ha ae yaw

hae,　　hae,　　tho-e　Wa - oo　ah-ma wae-tha-he - ba hoo-zhae -

wa - h'te ma-theum main - tae Hae-gaw　ah-wae ah-hae hae　Thae - thu wah -

pa - thin　h'te mum-b'thin ah-thin-hae hoo ah - wae　yaw　hae yaw.

No. 59. **MEKASEE.**

Heah   e   yaw   ha   ah   heah   e   yaw   ha   ah

Con ped.

heah   e   yah   ha   heah   e   yaw   ha   ah   wae   tha   hae

hae   tho   e   We - tun - gae - dae   sae - sa - sa   an - thun-

wan - ge - hae ya   he ah   e yaw   ha   wae ah   hae   tho.

No. 60.   MEKASEE.

Heah ha ah ha e ah ha e yaw heah ha ah ha ee yaw ee yaw

ee yaw ha e yaw heah ha ah ha ee yaw ee yaw ee yaw ah ha ee yaw

hae   hae   tho-e.   Me - ka-see ah-ma ma-zhon num - pa

ba-zhe ba   hae - ge - mun Heah ha ah ha ee yaw ee - gaw

ee - yaw ah ha ee - yaw hae hae yaw Ah ha e ya

ha e ya ah ha ah ha ee - yaw ee - yaw ee - yaw ha e yaw

Ah ha ah ha ee yaw ee yaw ee yaw ah ha ee yaw ha he yaw.

No. 61. NA-G'THE WA-A*N*.

Martial. ♩ = 72.

Ae - deun - ga - thae - tae tho Hae! Ka - gae

Con Ped.

No. 62. NA-G'THE-WA-A*N*.

Um-ba e - dan nan-koo-thae hun-thin-be-ga umba e - dan

nan-koo-thae hu*n* -thin-be -ga Hai! Nu-da*n* hu*n*-ga *ah-ah- je ah-ma-ta ah-an-*

tae ah-yae-zha-ma- tho Um-ba e - dan nan-koo-thae hu*n*-thin-be -ga.

No. 63. NA-G'THE WA-A*N*

Solemnly.

E - bae-ta*n* thin-gae- tho E - bae - tan thin-gae - tho

. . E-bae - ta*n* -thin-gae - tho . . Hae I*s*h - ah-ga-ma wa-gu*n*-za-be-dan

No. 63a. ## NA-G'THE WA-A*N*.

(Another version by Mr. La Flesche.)

No. 64. WAE-TO*N*-WA-A*N*.

Hu e tha ae he thae Hu e tha ae ha ae he thae thae

he thae thae Nu - da - hun-ga ke wa-shu - shae sna yae ae -

de - he - ke wa-shu - shae Hu e tha ae he thae Hu e

tha tha ha ae he thae thae he thae thae.

No. 65. WAE-TO*N*-WA-A*N*.

Ka-gae tae - he ha - ee thu*n* - zha ka-gae tae - he ha - ee thu*n* - zha Hae ish - ah - gae wa-gan-za - be - da*n* nu tae tae - he ha - ee thu*n* - zha, ka - gae tha - thu*n* - ga ta - du*n* shu*n* - tha - the - shae.

No. 66. WAE-TON-WA-AN.

Song. ♩ = 88. Drum. ♪ = 176.
With feeling.

Heah e tha ae he thae thae . . Heah e tha ae

Drum. pp

Con Ped.

ha ah ae he e thae . . Ae - de -he -ke

wa - shu - shae . . Heah e tha ae he thae thae

Heah e tha ae ha oh ae he e thae. . .

No. 67. WAE-TON-WA-AN.

♩. = 56. With marked rhythm.

Ou - hae - ke - tha - mae Wa - ba - ska - ha gha - gae wa - tha -

Con Ped.

stan-zheah-dan-hae   Ke - tha - mae Ou-hae - ke - tha - mae.

No. 68.   PONCA SONG.

♩ = 100.

E yah hae   ah hae thae   hae   thae   ah   ha thae hae   thae

Con Ped.

e yah hae   ah hae tha hae   hae   ah hae   thae hae tho-e

Ou - ke-tae-ah -ma   the-nun -un - ta - yae wash-kan- ae-gun - yah -hae

E   yah hae   ah   hae thae hae   hae   ah   hae   thae hae tho.

No. 69. WAE-WA-CHEE.

M.M. ♩ = 63.

Ah hae thae hae, ah hae thae hae Ah hae thae hae, ah hae thae hae Ah he he ae ha hae

Ped.

ae ah hae hae tho-ie: Sha - an - zhin-ga shon - gae the - ta

ou-da ho - wa - ne Ah hae thae ah hae ah hae thae hae tho.

No. 70. WAE-WA-CHEE.

Double beat.

He aw Tha ha hae ya hae hae aw tha ha thoe He aw tha ha

Con Ped.

hae ya hae yah hae thae he yae tha ha Oo-tha-zha-zhae-gan in- tae-dae

tha-gha-gae *he yae thae hae tho-e* Ou - thadaeou-the-shon we-snahte un-wan-shushae

He yah tha ha Ou-tha-zha-zhae-gan intae-dae tha-gha-gae *he yah tha ha tho.*

No. 71.   **WAE WACHEE.**

Double beat ♪ = 152.

Yae ha hae   *ya ae hae tha yae ha hae*   *ya ae hae tha*   *ah ha*   *ya ae hae tha*

Con Ped.

yae ha hae   *ya ae hae tha*   *tha ha tho-e* Zan-zhemundae ahma sha-ee   thae

ah   *ha*   *ya ae hae tha*   *ae ha hae*   *yae ae ha tha*   *tha ha tho.*

No. 72. WAE-WA-CHEE.

Double drumbeat. ♪ = 126.

He ya hae thae hae e ya hae he ya hae thae hae e ya hae

Con Ped.

he ya ha thae hae e ya hae hae ah hae thae hae tho-e Sha-an

zhin-ga na ae-ge-zhan-dan ae-ge-ma *tho* aeah-tan tha-ha-gae-ah *hae*

e ya hae thae hae e ya hae hae ah hae thae hae tho.

NOTE. Mr. La Flesche prefers this song in the key of C, with the last four measures in F.

No. 73. OMAHA PRAYER.

Grave, Solemn.

mp

Wa-kan-da thae-thu wah-pa-thin ah-tun-hae. Wa-kan-da thae-thu wah-pa-thin ah-tun-hae.

No. 74. HORSE MYSTERY SONG.

Nun-gae sha-tha-ma Nun-gae sha-tha-ma Shon-gae we-ta pa-

hun-ga thin ae-ah-ma Nun-gae sha-tha mae *tho hae.*

No. 75. IN-G'THAN WA-AN.

E - ka - gae dae e - ah- ma E - ka - gae dae e - ah - ma *Ah hae*

Con Ped.

ae ta-wan g'thun ma e - ah - ma *Ah hae tho-e.* Wa-kan -

da ma e - ah - ma *hae* ae Wa-kan-da ma e - ah-ma *Ah hae tho.*

138

No. 76. IN-G'THAN WA-AN.

No. 77. IN-G'THAN WA-AN.

No. 78. BUFFALO MYSTERY SONG.

Thae-thu - tan thae - ah-thae, Thae-thu-tan thae-ah - thae Thae-thu-tan thae-ah-thae thae-ah

thae Ae-gan ne-thun thae-ah - thae dun-ah - ma shan-ah-dun thae-ah-

Long hold.

thae Ae-gun thae-thu-tun thae-ah-thae shun thae - ah thae.

No. 79. MYSTERY SONG.

Du-da - ha man-thin *do he tho Ho he tha ha*

No. 80. **SONG OF THANKS.**

Slowly. **SOLO.** (No Accompaniment.)

Ha ae tha hae   ah hae thae hae we tha hae   ah hae thae hae   ae ahe hae thae

hae   tho   ah hae   hae   thae thoe   (name of don - or given.)

tha-un-tha-thae win-thae-kae ah hae thae hae ae tho ah hae thae hae ae tho ah hae thae hae tho

No. 81.   MYTH SONGS FOR CHILDREN.

HOW THE RABBIT LOST HIS TAIL.

♩ = 76.

Ma-stin-gae shae - tha-thin-shae win - jae - ga - tha - thin - shae,

win - jae - ga - tha - thin - shae   oh   hae   ya   hae   ya

hae   ya - hae   ya   wa - na -hae-tha -ba   wa - na -hae-tha - ba.

No. 82.   WA-OO WA-AN.

♩ = 76.

Nu - dan tha-g'the - dan   Ae   taeun   tha-thae - thae   Nu -

Con Ped.

dan tha-g'the   dan   Ae-taeun - tha-thae - thae   Nu- dan tha-g'the -

dan.   Ae - taeun - tha-thae-thae   ya   tha   ya   hi   Ha   tha

(64)

ha tha Nu-dan snae-tae-de wa - kan-da wae - ka - tun - hae *thae* Wa-

kan - da ae - haeah tun-hae *thae* ae-taeun-tha-thae-tha *ya tha ya hi.*

No. 83. WA-OO WA-A*N*.

♩ = 60.

Con Ped.

Ta-wu*n*-g'thu*n* thae-nun-yae - dae un-thu*n*-ge - ah thu*n*-kae thae

Wa-kan-da hae-ge-mu*n*-tae He-thin-ga-yae ga - ma he - ah - mae *hi.*

No. 84.   WA-OO WA-A**N**.

Thae-thu-ta*n* sha-tha-yae   thae-thu-ta*n* sha-tha yae   we-tu-zho*n*-gae e - ae tha-pe-ba

Con Ped.

ha*n*-wa*n*-ke-ah yae   thae--thu-ta*n* sha-tha yae   Wa-ha*n*-thin-gae e-

ae tha-pe-ba   ha*n* - wa*n*-ke-ah   yae   thae- thu -ta*n* sha - tha yae.

No. 85.   WA-OO WA-A**N**.

♩ = 58.

Du-de-ha u*n*-dum-bae nuz-zhi*n*-ga   Du-de-ha u*n*-dum-bae nuz-zhi*n*-

ga   ae - thum-bae ah - ya - nuz -zhin - dan   the-shna ou-we -

b'the-he - dae tha *hi*   *ah*   *ha*   Een-u-dan muz-zeah tun-hae thae

Een-u-dan muz-zheah tun-hae thae   Kan - zae-zhin-ga Een-u-dan muz-zheah tun-hae

ᴗhae   Pon - ca - ta   un - ga-thae-tae tha *tha*   *hi*.

No. 86. BE THAE-WA-AN.
LOVE SONG.

With expression. ♩ = 104.

He tha ho ha he ah hae ha hae he ah hae ah hae ha

Con Ped.

ho ho he tha hae he tha ha tha he ha ha tha ha

ha ah ha ah ho wae hae tho-e He tha ho ha he ah hae hae ha

hae hae he ah hae ah hae ha hae ha he tha hae tho.

No. 87. BE-THAE WA-AN.

LOVE SONG.

♪ = 80. *Smooth and flowing.*

Con Ped.

No. 88.   BE-THAE WA-A**N**.

No. 89.   BE-THAE WA-AN.

LOVE SONG.

♪ = 120.   *Light and joyous, smoothly.*

No. 90.   BE-THAE-WA-AN.
LOVE SONG.

Flowingly, with feeling.

𝅝 = 48.

Con Ped.

No. 91. FLAGEOLET PIECE.

No. 92. FLAGEOLET PIECE.

APPENDIX.

If the question should be asked, why in my notation of the songs here presented, I have not attempted to express certain peculiarities of intonation observable in Indian singing, I would simply say, that, during the earlier years of my studies, I was, with other observers, inclined to believe in the theory of a musical scale, in which the interval of a tone was divided into many parts; but, for several years now past, having become more familiar with the Indian's mode of thought and feeling concerning music, and as the result of careful investigation of hundreds of songs which I have transcribed, I have been led to account for his peculiar intonations in other ways than in the use of a minutely divided scale.

Upon page 11 I have called attention to the Indian's management of his voice, to his lack of ear training due to the absence of a standard pitch, and also to the influence upon his voice of out-of-door singing. Professor Fillmore on page 69 has spoken more fully upon this subject. I have also mentioned the Indian's fondness for the effect produced by vibrations of his voice. He uses various kinds of tremolo in his attempts at expression. For instance, a man, when accepting the gift of a horse, will render his song of thanks as if he were singing it while riding the animal; his notes will be broken and jarred in pitch, as if by the galloping of the horse. Or, as in the Mekasee songs, the warrior will so manage his voice as to convey the picture of the wolf trotting or loping over the prairie. Then again, the expression of emotions of mystery, or dread, seems to require the notes to be broken. If, when I was learning one of these songs, I held a quarter or half note to a steady tone, I was corrected and told to "make it tremble." It has not always been easy for me to distinguish between a tremolo used for expression, and a series of short notes; I have many times been set right by the Indian when I have mistaken a tremolo for thirty-second notes. In trying to express religious fears, or stress of emotion, the Indian is apt to slur from the pitch; he seldom attacks a note clearly.

In noting these songs I have been careful to present them truthfully, and they have been accepted by the Indian as correct. To convey Indian mannerism would be impossible, and any attempt to do so by a fanciful notation would end in caricature. These mannerisms do not form an integral part of the Indian's music, he is unconscious of them. It is easy to be caught in the meshes of these external peculiarities of a strange people, but if one would hear Indian music and understand it, one must ignore as he does his manner of singing.

ALICE C. FLETCHER.